'The Maitlands provide a brave, retrospective recount of a socially sensitive topic; the book's strength lies in the powerful nature of its dual perspective. An honest and touching approach with advice grounded in invaluable, personal experience. *Out of the Madhouse* is an excellent exploration of the phenomenology of mental illness and its wider impact.'

– Joshua Fletcher, psychotherapist and author of
Anxiety: Panicking about Panic

'This reflective book presents Michael's recovery from the multiple clinical effects emanating from abject low self-worth and loneliness. Whilst both traditional treatment as well as self-help and lifestyle strategies have helped him, the overriding ingredients that stand out in making positive change and enhancing resilience are the warmth of his connections, both family and friends, and the power of communication – spoken, written and art.'

– Dr Nihara Krause, Consultant Clinical
Psychologist, Founder and CEO, stem4

'*Out of the Madhouse* confronts the shocking bleakness of mental illness head on. Michael's diary of his battle to equip himself with both the tools and the will required to re-join something approaching mainstream existence is sobering... and Iain's tips and explanations are a big positive.'

– Charlie Mortimer, author of Dear Lupin *and* Lucky Lupin

of related interest

We're All Mad Here
The No-Nonsense Guide to Living with Social Anxiety
Claire Eastham
Foreword by Natasha Devon MBE
ISBN 978 1 78592 082 0
eISBN 978 1 78450 343 7

A Parent's Guide to Defeating Eating Disorders
Spotting the Stealth Bomber and Other Symbolic Approaches
Ahmed Boachie and Karin Jasper
ISBN 978 1 84905 196 5
eISBN 978 0 85700 528 1

A Short Introduction to Helping Young People Manage Anxiety
Carol Fitzpatrick
ISBN 978 1 84905 557 4
eISBN 978 0 85700 989 0
Part of the *JKP Short Introduction* series

Can I tell you about Depression?
A guide for friends, family and professionals
Christopher Dowrick and Susan Martin
Illustrated by Mike Medaglia
ISBN 978 1 84905 563 5
eISBN 978 1 78450 003 0
Part of the *Can I tell you about...?* series

OUT
OF THE
MADHOUSE

**AN INSIDER'S GUIDE TO
MANAGING DEPRESSION AND ANXIETY**

**MICHAEL MAITLAND
AND
IAIN MAITLAND**

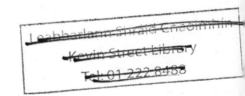
Jessica Kingsley *Publishers*
London and Philadelphia

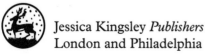

First published in 2018
by Jessica Kingsley Publishers
73 Collier Street
London N1 9BE, UK
and
400 Market Street, Suite 400
Philadelphia, PA 19106, USA

www.jkp.com

Library of Congress Cataloging in Publication Data
A CIP catalog record for this book is available from the Library of Congress

British Library Cataloguing in Publication Data
A CIP catalogue record for this book is available from the British Library

ISBN 978 1 78592 351 7
eISBN 978 1 78450 687 2

Printed and bound in Great Britain

In memory of Paul Di Carlo

Contents

Preface

Out of the Madhouse tells the story of Michael Maitland, and that of his family – dad Iain, mum Tracey, younger sister Sophie and younger brother Adam, plus Bernard the family dog.

Michael went to university in 2007 to do a degree in Illustration and, whilst there, he suffered from depression and anxiety which led eventually to anorexia and, finally, hospital and the Priory.

That's where our story begins, in the Priory in the late autumn of 2012. It is a story with a mix of happy and sad times, highs and lows – and tragedy. The story comes to an end in 2017.

The book is divided into three parts – Into the Priory, Going Home and Inside the Maitland Family. Michael's diary and notes form the backbone of much of the book and let fellow sufferers and their parents and loved ones see inside the head of someone with mental illness and understand how they think and feel.

Alternating with Michael's words, I write about the effects upon and feelings of the family – if you have a loved one with mental illness, you are not alone and will recognise much of what our family experienced over the years. I also offer self-help thoughts and ideas through the book that will help those with mental health issues, and those who love them, to manage depression and anxiety and related issues.

This is a memoir, a self-help guide and more – happiness, sadness, stupidity, regret, pain, shame, embarrassment and so many other emotions are all here. So too is love – angry, frustrated, irritated, worried and more – but always love. It is a strong and golden thread that runs from the start, right the way through to the end, and beyond.

Iain Maitland

P.S. With one or two exceptions, we have anonymised the names and slightly changed the details of everyone referred to in the book, other than the main Maitland family: Iain, Tracey, Michael, Sophie and Adam and Bernard the dog.

A FAIRY STORY

Once upon a time, not so very long ago, there was a nice family called the Maitlands who lived in a lovely house by the sea in Suffolk. Iain, the father, was a writer. Tracey, the mother, was a teaching assistant at a local primary school. They had three children – Michael, Sophie and Adam – and a Jack Russell dog named Bernard.

Iain spent 30 years writing books and articles, mostly on business and finance but also on health, wealth and happiness – articles such as 'Swop Your Cheese & Tomato Sandwich for £30,708', 'How to Make Someone's Eyes Pop Right Out of Their Head' and 'Men! Restore a Full Head of Hair with a Hot Fresh Cowpat'.

Tracey's work at the local primary school involved spending time with small, usually sweet and sometimes noisy, children between the ages of five and eight years. She occasionally had to dress up as historical figures, such as a pirate or a serving wench. She also made regular appearances as 'Where's Wally'. There were always copious amounts of paperwork to complete and meetings and stuff like that. There was plenty of wee, poo and sick at times as well.

Michael had a happy childhood, full of family fun, lots of friends and days out and holidays galore. He had a love of art, and a talent for it, from an early age. Having got a stack of GCSEs at Ipswich School and four A Levels at Northgate

Sixth Form College in Ipswich, Suffolk, he did a degree in Illustration in Norwich in 2007. He went on to begin a master's degree in Moving Image and Sound in 2011.

Sophie's childhood was equally happy. She was Head Girl at Amberfield, an all-girls school in Nacton, Suffolk, and then won a scholarship to go to Ipswich School to do her A Levels. She too got plenty of GCSEs and A Levels and went to Durham University to do a degree in Psychology from 2011 to 2014.

Adam, eleven years younger than Michael, and seven years younger than Sophie, was at Amberfield until he was seven and then moved to Ipswich School. With Michael having left home in 2007 and Sophie leaving in 2011, Iain, Tracey and Adam were a close, tight-knit family along with Bernard the dog.

Bernard lived on a farm with a farmer and his wife and daughters for the first four years of his life. Niamh, who owned Bernard, went to university with Michael as boyfriend and girlfriend. Bernard came to live with the Maitlands in 2008. For a long time, Adam and Bernard were constant companions.

One evening in October 2012, Iain received a text from Michael's girlfriend, Niamh. She texted that Michael had been taken to hospital with pneumonia and a collapsed lung. Anorexic, after years of anxiety and depression, he was on the brink of death.

So, what with that and one thing and another, the Maitlands didn't live happily ever after – at least, not for a very long time. In fact, there were times when they thought they'd never be happy again.

Part One

INTO THE PRIORY

November 2012
First thoughts

I'm being transferred from Ipswich Hospital to the Priory in Chelmsford (Essex). I'm dreading it, being away from Niamh and my life. But I know that if I don't go in, I'll probably be sectioned. If I go in voluntarily, I'm more likely to get out faster. I'm hoping I won't be in for more than a couple of weeks.

I've decided to keep a diary whilst I'm there. I've been told (by several health professionals) that it's a good thing for me to do and will help pass the time. I don't mind the first bit. The second sounds ominous. It's been suggested that I start writing by explaining how I got to this point.

I can't really believe how I managed to get this bad. At university (2007–2010), I slowly started to notice I didn't feel right. I began staying in more, not seeing people, and struggled with how I felt about myself. As my self-esteem dropped, so did my confidence and happiness, and I had quite a short temper at times.

University work (BA Illustration) became harder to do, and doing art was something that I've always loved doing. I've drawn, painted and taken photos for as long as I can remember, but I couldn't even bring myself to do any of that. I tried now and again to do things I enjoyed, but they just seemed to slip away from me. If you lose passion for something, then what's the point?

I felt like I had lost all my purpose and drive. This dragged me down further and I started hiding away and not seeing friends. I only saw my family very occasionally because I was with my girlfriend, Niamh, in a flat in Norwich 40-50 miles from where they lived. Things were mostly okay-ish between us but they did get difficult at times. Generally, Niamh was always happy and had plenty of drive (and supported and encouraged me as best she could), whereas I found it hard to even get up out of bed at times.

After university (2010), we moved back to Ipswich and this was when things got really bad. I didn't see anyone any more, rarely left the house and wouldn't talk to anyone, apart from Niamh, for days on end. It was then I think I started to feel like there was a big hole inside of me, like part of me had died. I didn't really care any more about anything – especially myself. I didn't care about my health, how I looked or the fact I was on my own for much of the time when Niamh was at work. I stopped doing what normal people would do to make themselves happy. I stayed in bed and wouldn't eat and never spent any money on myself.

Once you start treating yourself like you're worthless, you start to think you are worth nothing and life can feel pretty pointless. Why get up if you have nothing, hate yourself and each day feels like a constant struggle? It's hard to describe how I felt, but each day was like a battle and I would hate waking up in the morning knowing I had to struggle through another day. I was lonely and inside I know

I'd given up hope of feeling happy again. I think I'd forgotten what it felt like.

I can see now that I've been suffering from anxiety and depression; at least, that's what the doctors tell me. I also have all sorts of other issues such as OCD. I don't like the way I look. I struggle to make decisions. I don't like change. It's all pretty endless. These all sort of turned into an eating disorder; I think that this was my way of controlling things. I did not mean to be anorexic. It just seemed to happen. People talk about my anorexia as if that's all there is to it. In a way, it's got nothing to do with weight loss at all. (It is about control.)

I began to get really thin and started feeling unwell all the time from about 2011. Towards the beginning of this winter (2012) I remember being really cold one day and then felt like I had a really bad bug. My breathing was very laboured and I started coughing up blood a lot. I vomited up large amounts of blood several times. I spent about a week walking around like this, just ignoring it as best I could.

I then woke up one morning and my whole body was swollen. I got up and looked in the mirror and I couldn't even recognise myself. I looked all fat and bloated, like something out of a horror movie. I was rushed to the hospital and was told I had oedema and my lung had collapsed and I was dying.

(I've been Googling 'oedema' and it's essentially this: 'Life-threatening infections or other critical illnesses can cause a reaction that allows fluid to leak into tissues almost everywhere. This can cause swelling all over the body.' Not good!)

I was in hospital for a while. I remember being in a room with old people. I don't know if they have a death ward in hospital where they put everyone who is going to die to keep them away from everyone else, but that's what it felt like to me. The people around me were all about to die. I think the old man next to me may have died whilst I was there. The staff raced in one day and drew the curtains round him and I didn't see him again. I often wondered if I was going to die there too.

Hospital was a horrible, isolating experience. I rarely saw a doctor. When they did come, they would bring trainee nurses to look at me like I was an exhibit in a freak show. I had various lung scans to see how bad my lungs were. My left lung had collapsed and was full of fluid that needed to be drained. The only way to do this was to put a long needle through my back and into my lung whilst I leaned forward. Niamh was there when they did this. I looked at Niamh's face and she looked horrified.

I was discharged from hospital because I think they needed the bed. I felt like I was dying. I was scared to leave to go home because at this point I was in a wheelchair, could barely walk and still felt like I was dying. When I got home, I couldn't even get up the stairs. I had to drag myself up using the banister. I couldn't wear shoes because my feet were swollen and double their size. They felt like size 19s.

I started having check-ups and the doctor was so shocked with how I was both physically and, I suppose, mentally that he referred me to a local critical patient team. They then suggested the Priory and said why don't I go there for a couple of weeks. They made it sound like a holiday, but I think that if I'd said no thank you very much, they would have taken me anyway.

So I've packed my bags and here I am ready to go into the loony bin.

I'm scared.

THIS IS HOW I SEE MYSELF. UGLY, EMPTY, DEAD.

On arrival

It's a freezing cold day. I'm sitting on my own in a room (in the Priory) waiting to see a nurse who's going to give me some sort of a check-up. I'm staring out of the window thinking how the hell it's all come to this. Niamh and her mum have been and gone, and I know I've messed things up really badly this time. I miss my home and already feel trapped in this strange place. My initial thoughts are that I want to get up, break through the window and leg it all the way back up the A12.

* * *

The nurse carried my bag into the room and emptied it on to the bed to search for anything and everything. She took away a large bag of items and objects that shouldn't be in there – even my fizzy drinks. I was then given my meal plan, which is actually far less than I would normally eat. The meal plan details the amount of food you will have each day and it will be stepped up depending on whether your weight is increasing enough or not. I'm already beginning to panic as I'm starting to realise what lies ahead. I feel I'm at rock bottom.

* * *

It's now the evening and I'm still sitting on the end of the bed feeling completely lost. I can't see how I'm going to adjust to living here. Today, my food has been a yoghurt and a bowl of fruit – way less than what I'm used to.

When Niamh left this morning, I watched her walking away and I knew I wasn't going to see her again for a long time. Deep down inside, I fear she's had enough and that this is the last time I will ever see her.

I'm thinking again about how I got here and wish that I'd tried harder to avoid this, but the reality is I had given up.

I'm going to have to meet the others in here soon and, having heard their shrieks and yells all day, I feel scared and unsure what to expect.

In the morning, I know I'm expected to sit and have breakfast with all of them. I haven't even had breakfast in years, let alone with others watching me. I'm also starting to realise that I could miss Christmas this year. I've always loved Christmas. I can't help thinking my Christmas Day will be spent here in this room on my own.

This place is killing me.

WHAT HAPPENED TO MICHAEL - AND US

So, where to begin the other (family) side of the story? If, as a parent, you have a child who has mental health issues to the point where they have been hospitalised and, to all intents and purposes, sectioned in what someone of my age (fifties) would call a 'mental institution', you can't help but feel a range of extreme emotions. Sadness, anger, frustration, disappointment, disbelief, heartbreak and, not least, guilt and a sense of failure as a parent and as a human being. You ask yourself, 'How did it ever get to this?'

One of the first things I did was to look back over everything that happened to see how Michael got to this place. With the benefit of hindsight, I can see his oh-so-slow decline – inch by inch at a time – from when he left to go to university in 2007 through to when he collapsed in October 2012. A long, long time – five years. For a while, it was so slow that we did not notice it. We were blind for almost all of it.

He lived with his girlfriend, Niamh, in a flat we'd bought in Norwich and they both did degrees at the University of the Arts. To us, he had everything anyone could ever want. His life should have been perfect. And we were a happy family, all getting along and doing well – it never occurred to us that anything bad could happen to any of us.

We saw Michael and Niamh regularly during their university years. We went up for meals out, at least early on. They came down and saw us. Weekends, Mother's Day, Father's Day, birthdays, days out. All much as it ever was. We went on holidays, to America and to Spain. Michael's appearance changed over this time: he grew slimmer, his hair changed colour time and again, he wore different clothes, had his ears pierced – nothing particularly out of the ordinary with any of that. He was growing up. And he was an art student, after all. He wasn't studying to be an accountant (thank goodness).

There were some tensions between us, especially as they came towards the end of their studies. We had paid out much – for the flat and 101 other things – and expected them now to get jobs and move into the real world and support themselves. They moved into a cottage back in Ipswich and...nothing much seemed to happen...for ages...and ages. I shouted. Cajoled. Threatened to withdraw financial support. None of it seemed to make a jot of difference. I thought, deep breath, Michael was a waste of space, a freeloader, a pain in the backside. There were moments when I would have been happy to never see him again. I didn't really think about mental health matters; it wasn't something that would happen to any of us. I just thought he wasn't a nice person.

The next two years are now something of a blur – these were tense days, months, years. On and on. Round and round. Down and ever downwards. Michael inching towards his demise. Michael and Niamh moved home two or three times, each to a slightly smaller and grottier place. There were still significant issues between us – I remember shouting, 'Is anyone anywhere ever going to do anything?' Niamh did get a job. Michael didn't. He stayed at home in bed, staring at the wall. There was a lot of anger from me towards him. I had many negative feelings.

As time passed, we slowly became aware that something wasn't quite right about him and that he was thinner. We did not know what to do. We did not want to confront him and thought we might lose all contact with him if we did. We looked the other way. We hoped for the best – that, somehow, whatever it was would come good.

It didn't – I remember getting the text, pretty much out of the blue, from Niamh that evening in October 2012. I caught my breath, on the brink. I texted back, 'Is it terminal?' A long, long pause. My heart cracking. About to text the same question again, in slightly different words: 'Is Michael dying?' As I slowly pressed the keys, another text arrived from Niamh, 'No'; it's not terminal. I did not know if it was the truth or a simple kindness. Either way, everything changed that night.

And so Michael went into hospital. We got updates; he had stabilised and was now steady-ish. He wasn't going to die, at least not now, not at any moment. I remember visiting him in hospital, seeing this once-handsome, six-foot boy who should have been in the prime of his life, slumped stick-like and empty-eyed in a wheelchair. A pitiful wretch. Another mix of emotions: pity, shame, embarrassment, awkwardness. How had it ever come to this without us seeing it all for what it was?

Michael left hospital and, not long after, we were told he was going into the Priory, as if it were no more than a short break to Llandudno. He had reached the end of his journey. We were relieved, not least because, having come face to face at last with this utter horror, we knew it had to be sorted fast, and we had no idea where we would have started resolving it.

Friday 30 November 2012

I woke up at 7am this morning and feel completely alone. I can hear distant shouting from other sections of the hospital. I'm about to head out for breakfast and wish Niamh was here alongside me. I don't want to talk to anyone and feel angry. I'm so angry because I've let myself get to this point and no one could help me.

I'm already getting severe headaches from caffeine withdrawal. I'm used to drinking a lot of coffee and we are only allowed decaf in here. The switch is noticeable and I'm only allowed one coffee with each meal – three very small cups of coffee a day.

* * *

The staff talk to you like you're a child and we are locked in a small unit with separate rooms. I have only met a handful of different staff members. Some seem more friendly than others, but I can imagine that looking after lunatics like me isn't much fun. We must never go into each other's rooms, and staff check up on me every 15 minutes to make sure I haven't made a run for it. I don't know where I'd go to, or even how I'd get out, but I would run if I could.

They even check when I'm going to the toilet. I'd obviously been in there too long today as the nurse suddenly shouted, 'Are you all right in there?' I answered, 'Hold on, I'm just trying to hang myself.' That really didn't go down too well, but it made me laugh for once. The rest of the time I just felt angry.

THE SIGNS WE SHOULD HAVE SPOTTED

I have put together a rough and ready list of tell-tale signs we should have spotted that revealed Michael was not well in the build-up to hospital and the Priory, and then grouped these under general headings in case you are now where we were all those years ago.

Look for patterns of changing behaviour

We knew that Michael, as he went through university, had stopped doing any outside work. He had a part-time job cleaning plates at a restaurant prior to that. He gave up the football and karate that he had loved to do for many years.

He also stopped seeing his friends, some of whom he'd known for ten or twelve years.

We saw all of that as Michael focusing on his degree – and having a live-in girlfriend too – but the benefit of hindsight suggests he was already cutting himself off from the outside world. That's very common with people with mental illness and something to watch for.

Sometimes, of course, these changing patterns of behaviour are natural; people grow up, move away, develop new interests and change, especially when they are free from the influences of their parents. They can become themselves. Sometimes these changes point towards something more worrying, though: depression, anxiety and other mental health matters. It's not always simple to tell the difference.

Watch for changes in demeanour

Michael has always been a quiet boy and it's not always easy to spot the difference between 'quiet happy' and 'quiet sad'. It may be easier to spot the difference with livelier, more vocal children. Sophie was a Tigger-ish teenager; we knew when she was happy and when she was angry and when she was sad. Shouting and slamming doors are easy signs to identify – a child who is essentially quiet and gentle, and kind of monotone, is harder to deal with in some respects.

Everyone is different, of course, but many parents talking about their children who have experienced mental illness list a range of issues to spot here: not talking any more, not sharing confidences and secrets as they once did, being snappy and short-tempered. 'Shutting themselves off' and 'closing in on themselves' are two phrases that come up regularly in conversations I have with many people who've been down this road. 'Subtle and not so subtle' changes in personality is another.

Keep an eye on physical changes

As mentioned, Michael's appearance changed over time: lots of different hairstyles, earrings, hats, clothes. We thought that – and the fact that he slimmed down so much – was part of growing up and losing his teenage chubbiness. And he was a student, and an art student at that, so we expected him to look a bit wacky.

We realised, before Michael was hospitalised, that he was not right and that he was thin, and we did not know what to do about it. We felt that if we confronted him and Niamh, he might turn away from us and we might lose him. So we just kept quiet – seriously, this is the worst thing to do *ever* – and hoped for the best. We did not see the tipping point between 'being thin' and 'becoming anorexic'.

Get close and stay close

Michael lived 40–50 miles away from us and, as he worsened, we saw him less and less, to the point where, eventually, he made his excuses to miss cinema trips and meals out on Mother's Days and Father's Days. When we did see him, and with Niamh ever bright and breezy, he just needed to rally ever so slightly to fool us into thinking that, if he was not quite well, he was not as close to death's door as he actually was. And, for much of the time, we weren't really looking anyway so we were easy enough to fool.

If you live with someone who you suspect has issues, it may be easier to spot the signs sooner. For depression, the most common tell-tale signs are, in no particular order: being restless, being edgy and agitated, loss of appetite, lack of energy, sense of tiredness and sleep-related issues. A sufferer may experience one or two or more of these. There are no set rules, but there will be some sort of changes.

Spot other changes

If you looked at a how-to text book – let's say a how-to text book on spotting depression and related issues – it would give you a whole long list of 'signs' to watch for. Examples? Low mood. Feeling down. Loss of concentration. Losing confidence. Feeling guilty… And many more. All correct and tickable off a checklist.

But it's often not that straightforward. Mental ill-health is messy and nasty, manipulative and devious; it does not fit easily into checklists and boxes to be ticked off one by one – job done, all sorted. Michael, for a long time, did not realise he was depressed. He had a 'low mood' because he had moved away from his home and family. That seemed natural enough. He 'felt down' because he was doing a degree in an unfamiliar city. Most people would struggle a little with that. It took him years – not months, but *years* – to realise he was actually suffering from depression.

It unfolded slowly until it took him over. Michael felt sad most of the time and lost interest in what he liked doing: drawing, painting, photography. This – and it's chicken and egg – rolled itself into always feeling anxious and worried about what might happen. He suffered from low self-esteem – feeling both hopeless and guilty – and this, mixed in with growing levels of irritation and anger, skewed his personality: edginess, a shortening temper, etc. Many people describe depression as a black dog; for us, it's more of a tentacled monster, with each tentacle entwined and overlapping – one is anxiety, another is depression, and OCD, and so on.

Most of this we simply did not see. We saw a quiet boy who went to university, lived in a nice flat, was supported by us, had a happy girlfriend, was doing a course he loved – all sorts of art every day – and was just growing up and changing and becoming his own person. Wonderful! What more could a parent ask for. Fact is, though, he was his own person – with anxiety and depression – which he disguised well enough and for long enough. The horror of it all only became apparent when he was taken to hospital. The signs were there, though. We should have seen them – or at least some of them.

Saturday 1 December 2012

Last night, I had vegetable kebabs for dinner and then Niamh turned up out of the blue to see me. I don't think I could do this without knowing I had her there waiting for me at the end of it all. I just don't think I could do it.

* * *

Meal times are really hard because we get told what to have for breakfast, but then for lunch and dinner we get to choose what we have for ourselves from a choice of three different meals. When my head is all over the place, it's hard for me to make choices. I can't come to any decision easily – it gives me panic attacks and I end up loathing myself and feeling guilty about that. It's a vicious circle.

* * *

The idea behind the meal plan is that it steps up each week, eventually to a point where you are being overfed, to quickly put on weight. I already miss my routines and ways of living. I just miss all the small and simple things that I took for granted, like the freedom to walk down the street or pop to the shop, being able to drive my car or be outside in the sunshine.

I'm not used to being around people either and I don't like talking at the moment. The staff are always trying to engage with me, but I don't want to talk and have nothing to say to them *at all*. I just feel broken and, no matter what they say to me, I feel dead inside.

* * *

Today I have a group session to do with body image. Hopefully, it will help me get a better understanding and try to find a way for me to think more positively. Body image is about how we view ourselves. It is about trying to address what we don't like about ourselves, which isn't always something obvious. Not many people in the world love their own body, but the people in this group probably all hate themselves and the way they look.

* * *

We talked about whether others influence the way we feel – friends, family, etc. Also, how the media and advertising can impact young people's outlook and the idea of what people should look like 'ideally'. There is a lot of pressure on teenagers to look a certain way: 'perfect'. The media has a lot to answer for.

THE THINGS WE SHOULD HAVE DONE

We are not experts in depression and related mental health issues, although we have lived through Michael's story and have learned much from it that we can share with you. There are things we should have done before Michael ended up in hospital and the Priory. If you have a loved one who you think suffers from mental ill-health, but perhaps does not realise it or want to address it yet, you may want to think about these ideas.

Be there

We were always there for Michael in our own way. But we never really believed what was happening to Michael was that bad; remember, we felt nothing like this could happen to a happy family like ours. As an aside, I should say at this point that depression and other mental illnesses can strike anyone anywhere any time. Male, female. Old, young. Gay, straight, transgender. Black, white. Rich, poor. It can be completely at random. There's often no obvious cause. There's no one to blame. Sometimes, bad stuff happens to good people. That's life – it is the way it is. You just have to get on with it.

As he became thinner and seemed out of sorts, we waited and assumed things would somehow come good. We were 'there' and helped Michael in all the practical ways – somewhere to live, money, making sure his car had an MOT –

and would have done something relating to his mental health issues had Michael said something. He never did. We should have seen it and addressed it anyway, though. That is a huge regret. We should have done something, been proactive.

If you think you see something wrong – your loved one seems to have changed personality in some way or to have lost all interest in something they used to love, for example – it's tempting, if not natural, as a parent to move in and sort it (bearing in mind you've probably sorted out almost everything for them for years and years). You may say something along the lines of 'You have a problem, this is what it is and here's how to sort it out.'

As a dad, my default response then (but not now) would have been to shout this. Tracey's approach would have been to talk around and around the matter before stopping and then starting all over again. Sophie's default mode would have been to shout too (probably louder and longer than me). Adam was eleven years Michael's junior and too young to do anything. We did not really have any extended family – a nice uncle or a friendly cousin – or close friends who could have taken us to one side and said, 'Have you noticed that Michael…?' or could have had a quiet word with Michael himself.

From what we've learned since, from talking to Michael and other parents and teenagers with similar stories, often a sympathetic rather than a practical response can be most effective. It's not a matter of confronting, emphasising, directing, leading or pushing someone to do something (however good you might think it is for them). It's more about just being there, empathising, listening, encouraging and helping them to find their own solution in their own way and time. (Obviously, in an emergency, you may have to take a more practical approach.)

Encourage them to talk

You – if you are Mum or Dad – may be a warm and loving parent, but that does not necessarily mean you are the best person to help in this situation, even though you may feel you love your child more than anyone else in the world and know them best of all. Michael felt ashamed and embarrassed about what was happening to him, and he didn't want to upset us at all. He talked to his girlfriend, Niamh, who protected him as best she could, including shielding him from us. Michael has also benefited from sharing his story with professionals who have suffered from depression like him.

At some point, someone suffering from mental illness – and it may take them some time to realise this – needs to talk about it to someone; it's pretty much the first step towards their eventual recovery. How you get them to talk and who does it – a big sister, a best friend, a family member who has had similar issues, a medical professional – can be tricky. Raising it head-on, however gently, may lead to anger and denials if it's too early; there may be tears of relief if the timing is right.

Somehow – and it's often gently and slowly does it – a conversation needs to begin. It can be effective to ask how they are and how they're feeling. You (or whoever is doing this) might want to mention you've noticed such-and-such (such-and-such being that they've stopped doing something they used to enjoy, for example). You need to try to get a sense of how open they are about this; remember, they may not have seen it for themselves yet.

It's wise to avoid putting whatever it is you've noticed (maybe signs of irritability, tearfulness) into the context of some sort of labelled illness – 'depression' or 'anxiety' or whatever. Too soon, too strong. It's also sensible to avoid telling, instructing or even suggesting – the sort of feeling, however well meant, that you can identify the issue, put it in a box and pack it away with just a simple chat. You have to go at their pace, and give them time and space – if they are not ready and you press them, they are more likely to become defensive.

Listen

My natural inclination with my children even now (although I have finally learned to curb it) is to identify their problem and then tell them what they need to do resolve it. I suspect that many parents, particularly fathers, are much the same; talking to teenagers these days, I often hear the same type of comments over and again. There is often a sort of sense of 'Dad's great, nice guy and all that, but he does tell me what to do all the time.' The phrase 'bull in a china shop' was used when I was young; it's appropriate here.

I do recall conversations, as Michael was starting to seem down and becoming thinner, when I offered a range of 'advice' along the lines of 'For God's sake, cheer up' and 'Eat something – put some meat on your bones.' None of these comments helped at all. Looking back, I can't imagine why I thought they would. I suppose shouting made *me* feel a little better but I can't think it was of much help to anyone else.

Getting the issue out in the open – to the point where the sufferer acknowledges it and wants to address it – has much to do with listening – to what they say, how they say it, when they want to say it. Had I realised Michael was struggling and raised it with him before he recognised it himself, I suspect the outcome would have worsened matters. Michael would have become defensive and hidden himself away more and I would have felt angry and frustrated. Having talked to parents and teenagers, there seems to come a point when the sufferer knows they are in difficulties. That's the moment to start the conversation ideally – not always easy if you can see them declining before you.

Get advice

Get professional help as soon as you can – NOW – even if it's just you rather than you and your loved one at this stage. We'll talk more about where to get help as we progress through the book. But at this point it is worth stating that although the formal and informal systems are often, in our experience, messy and tangled and rather hit and miss, there is a lot of help out there. You may have to work a little to find it. (We'll help you with that later on.)

Your GP is a good place to start. Michael had mixed experiences with GPs – generally, as he went through one after the other for help, they offered him pills and different pills and fewer pills and more pills – but always pills, pills, pills. He felt that none of them – possibly because they had no direct personal experience of mental illness themselves – really understood or engaged with him at all. But these days, we are told that every practice has someone who focuses on mental health. GPs also offer a signposting service to self-help groups in the local community, for example. That's invaluable.

You may find that there are many self-help groups locally, perhaps for eating disorders or depression, that are run by volunteers who have personal experience of these issues. For Michael, someone who has had the same issues as him understands him. Someone who has all the paper qualifications in the world and as many letters after their name as you can fit on a page but who has never suffered mental ill-health does not really understand him. Simple as that.

I suppose it is a little bit like a pregnant woman who goes to see her GP. If that GP is a man, he can say all the right things, and offer good advice, and generally be very useful. But he has never personally experienced pregnancy, labour and childbirth so, when push comes to shove, he doesn't really *know* in quite the same way that a female GP would who has had children herself.

If I had to summarise 'what to do', it's really a matter of being there, ready to talk and listen, and, in the meantime, getting help from your GP – you may be feeling stressed and anxious because of this (so take care of yourself too) – and talking to local people with personal experience via self-help groups. They will almost certainly talk to you, offer a shoulder to lean on, share thoughts and ideas. They will understand.

Sunday 2 December 2012

Last night, Niamh came to see me. It is a 100-mile round trip and she only has an old car and not much money really. She made me a Christmas tree to have in my room. She has always tried to help me and do the best for me, I've been very lucky. We got to hang out for a bit, but I felt crap. I feel like my life is over and I don't know how to change the way I think. I've tried so many different things and ways to overcome this but nothing ever works for me. It's why I've ended up here.

I've tried going to about four or five different GP surgeries, which never really worked for me because they don't quite know what to do with someone like me. They can offer pills and I've tried quite a few different ones. The one I'm on currently is called citalopram. It can work for some people but I don't like being on pills or having to rely on them. I don't think it's right for someone to have to take a pill that makes them numb or, worse, want to kill themselves.

I've tried cognitive behavioural therapy (CBT), which again can be useful if you're open to the idea. CBT can be used to treat people with a range of mental health problems. It's all about how we think, the actions we take and how we feel. So, obviously, if you're thinking negatively then the most likely outcome or outlook is going to be negative. If you're in an awful place, it can sometimes be hard to focus your mind on change. Some people don't want to get better or, like me, have given up completely.

* * *

Today for breakfast, I had Weetabix and for lunch I'm having fruit and custard which is seriously weird. Well, it seems weird to me that that's my lunch. Of all the things they could give me, they chose that. Why would anyone do that?

* * *

I was weighed this morning and have come in at a whopping 45 kilos. At this point I don't even know how I feel about that. At least I can say I've achieved something not many people can do. You have to have determination or in my case such self-hatred to get to that.

* * *

Today was kind of productive. I lay in bed and watched the entire *Lord of the Rings* trilogy back to back. Then for dinner I had a Spanish omelette before heading back to my room to cry – at least I have a new routine to get into.

I don't really sleep very well here. Partly because I get checked on every 15 minutes. Also, being weighed in the early hours of the morning doesn't help.

It's difficult to sleep when I'm always on edge and my mind is always ticking. Thinking about the next weigh-in and wanting to go home. It's all over the place.

ANGER EXERCISE 1: SNAPPING THE CANE

This book is part memoir, part how-to. We want to share Michael's story – the family's too – from beginning to end so that you can see how it feels to suffer from mental illness – to be inside Michael's head for a while – and to experience what it's like, albeit at arm's length, as part of the family. Mental illness, after all, does not just affect the sufferer but their partners, parents, brothers and sisters, wider family and friends to varying degrees. It causes misery, breaks relationships and can pretty much ruin everything, at least for a while.

At the same time, we want to offer some 'how-to' – not exactly advice and guidance as such, as we are just ordinary folk rather than professionals with lots of qualifications and years of expertise. But we offer our thoughts and ideas for you to consider – some of these may help you and your loved ones; others won't but may suit other people. That's the way of mental health. It's your call.

As Michael raises various issues such as anger, stress and anxiety in his diary, we are going to offer practical suggestions of things to do. We are going to drop in one or two at a time rather than give you page after page of, say, anger management techniques. We don't want to break the flow of Michael's story too much now we've got underway. Nor do we want to turn this into a text book.

The self-help exercises we're suggesting for anger, stress, anxiety and so on are all easy to do. Clearly, though, these are low-level, especially in Part One of our story, and you are not going to turn severe anxiety or clinical depression around by, as we'll see in a moment, something like snapping a cane or breathing deeply. But we need to start somewhere and the beginning is always a good place, and we will look at more heavy-duty things later in the book.

Cane snapping, and variations of it, is an anger management exercise that's been around for a good while. You stand up and hold a cane or a thin piece of wood in your hands (not too thick, and you'll see why in a minute).

Hold this out in front of you. At the same time, bring your knee up and the cane down sharply so that it snaps. You may wish to shout out, as loudly as you can, whilst you do this. Repeat until you feel the anger ease.

Variations include using an imaginary cane – often easier, unless you have a constant supply of canes – and holding your fists in front of your face, bringing them down quickly to your sides as you shout or grunt or make some other noise. The key point is that you make some sudden, almost violent, gesture and that this, with loud shouting, can blow that anger away. It's a quick fix that's effective for some people.

Monday 3 December 2012

It feels like I'm in prison as we get marched single file through locked corridors, escorted by members of staff with walkie-talkies. The others seem extremely thin to me and I feel normal, but I know deep down I'm probably the most mental of all of them. I know I'm thin too really, but I look at the others and to me they look way worse than me, but I know it's hard for me to see what I'm really like.

My head is always playing games with me, telling me I'm a worthless person but also that I shouldn't be here. It's hard to know what to think any more. I think about Niamh a lot. Today is the anniversary of when we met and we don't get to see each other because Dr Webster said she couldn't come today because I need to focus, whatever the hell that means. What am I supposed to be focusing on exactly?

My meal plan has been stepped up. I'm now eating way more than I would at home and I feel awful. I'm spending most of my day feeling stuffed and at the point of vomiting. I also have a constant headache. The days drag so slowly.

You start to realise what you're missing from real life – even the smallest things like going for walks, lying in my own bed, seeing my family or going to the cinema. The only thing keeping me going at the moment is knowing that I get to see Niamh most evenings.

Tomorrow I'm having a proper lunch, not cold stodgy custard with soggy fruit. I also know that my meal plan is stepping up again soon as my weight is so low. I think I weigh less than most of the girls here and I'm about six foot.

Tuesday 4 December 2012

I've just had a meeting with the head nurse who said I'm lucky to be here and by all accounts I could very easily have died. That's nice, isn't it? She said that I'm one of the most shocking cases she has seen and she is surprised I've made it this far. So much for the pep talk.

I'm really starting to panic now as the food is being increased again. It's getting to the point where it's becoming unmanageable, but they keep telling me that I need to do it or my body could shut down.

I have something for breakfast, lunch and dinner along with a snack. The amounts of puddings and number and sizes of snacks are increasing.

It's relentless!!!

The atmosphere here is so claustrophobic and unsettling. The addicts are in the next corridor and I have talked to a couple when I've passed them in the dining hall. I have already spoken to staff and said I want to leave. I have no option but to stay, though. I could make a run for it but I know that wouldn't end well.

Another group session: bloody yoga. I felt like a complete idiot and being the only man there made things even worse. Even though I felt awkward, I did actually feel slightly more relaxed. It didn't take long, though, before I returned to my room and fell back into hell. I hate being here. I feel so lonely and lost. Sitting alone in my room makes me realise how far I've fallen. I'm in prison, really.

Wednesday 5 December 2012

Today, I'd had enough and refused to get up. I was set on staying in bed all day, but the nurses came in and forced me up. I got angry and said stuff I shouldn't have. I don't normally swear or lose my temper, but when I'm pushed I can snap sometimes. Being treated like a child for so long pushed me too far. The nurses tried to talk me down and told me to relax. It's easy enough saying that but when you're in this place, living like this, it's too easy to crack.

Eventually, when I had got up and dressed, they left me alone and I pulled back the curtains and saw it was snowing. It made me realise how trapped I am in here.

* * *

This morning I got weighed and came in at 44.1 kilos, whatever that is. The snow is getting pretty heavy outside and I'm starting to realise Niamh might not be able to make it here tonight. It's hard to write stuff down sometimes as the days all merge into one big black mess where you sit around thinking about how crap everything is.

I have chosen the meals I will be having today. For lunch, beans on toast for what seems like the 100th time. For dinner, vegetable kebabs (again).

* * *

At this moment, lunchtime, I'm sitting on the edge of the bath with the door locked trying not to cry. Tomorrow, I get to speak to Dr Webster. He is the head guy who oversees everyone and ultimately has the final say on everything. The meetings with him are few and far between and are make or break really – basically, it's my chance to pretend to be normal, so let's not do anything mental or say I want to jump off the Orwell Bridge. These talks happen on a Thursday. We are called in one-by-one at any point during the day. It lasts around ten minutes.

I'm also meeting a guy called Richard this afternoon, who does CBT. Richard focuses on teaching me on how the mind works and how it can be trained to think differently – more positively. I will then have a body image class where we all sit around and talk about how we feel and why we hate ourselves – all good fun. We are a relatively small group of weirdos, so it's a chance for us to see how each of us are suffering. I don't really like talking about myself to others.

* * *

I just spoke to Richard (the CBT guy). He is awesome and has begun to explain to me how CBT can help change the way I think and see different situations. He told me about something called the hippocampus in the brain. This can shrink when you become depressed but can also be trained to function properly. I like him because he's the only person that doesn't talk to me like I'm a five-year-old. We can actually talk like mates. He also tried to help put things into perspective for me and I think he might be able to help me. Richard talks a lot about thought patterns and trying to bring back a more positive and balanced outlook on situations and life.

* * *

I'm feeling really desperate and want to speak to Dr Webster. I feel desperate because getting to talk to him is very rare and I know he's my only way out of here at the end of the day. I have to try to seem calm and collected when I talk to him but inside I'm screaming, 'I want to get out.' Got to just play this game to get out. I feel like I'm in the Hunger Games. I'm starting to hate the amount of food I have to eat.

I'm worried about Niamh driving in the snow. I look forward to her getting here but it almost makes things worse once she leaves and I realise how bad it is here. I'm starting to feel like I won't ever know what it's like to be happy again.

If you think about it, what is happy?

All I know is I feel crap and the worst I've felt in a long time. Being happy, in my mind, is being comfortable with who you are, enjoying your life and feeling connected to what is around you at the present moment. I feel none of these things.

* * *

I haven't been happy for so long. No matter what pills I take, I still end up feeling like this. I've tried fluoxetine and many others, but right now I'm on a high dosage of citalopram. Pills can have an effect on me – they make me numb, care a little less about anything and make me tired. If I stop taking them, I pretty much feel like killing myself, it can be that bad. I don't want to take pills, though. I'm trapped either way.

I'm also stressed about seeing my family soon. I'm ashamed that I'm here and for them to see me in this situation. I miss my brother and sister. I don't think my parents want Adam to see me here and to see me looking such a mess. I clearly look mental, skeletal and surrounded by some pretty shocking-looking people. I can't even begin to explain how much I miss the outside world. I haven't had fresh air in ages now.

Me and my meds

I wanted to write down the medications I had taken before going into the Priory:

Fluoxetine (Prozac, Sarafem)

Fluoxetine is used to treat different types of depression, obsessive compulsive disorder, some eating disorders and panic attacks.

The more common side effects of this drug can include strange dreams, decreased sexual desire, erectile dysfunction (trouble getting or keeping an erection) and decreased appetite. Side effects can also include trouble sleeping, anxiety, rash, sweating and diarrhoea.

In some cases, fluoxetine can cause serious side effects. These side effects can include serotonin syndrome, mania, low salt levels, abnormal bleeding and seizures.

Citalopram (Celexa)

This drug and other antivepressant drugs may increase suicidal thoughts or actions in some children, teenagers or young adults within the first few months of treatment or when the dose is changed.

Trazodone (Oleptro)

In some cases, trazodone can cause serious side effects. These include thoughts of suicide. This risk is higher for children, teens and young adults within the first few months of treatment.

ANGER EXERCISE 2: BREATHING IN POSITIVES

Anger was something that was almost overwhelming Michael in these early days in the Priory. It's a common thread and an issue that many readers may relate to. One of the things that Michael did to manage it, eventually, was breathing exercises. These are so simple but often brilliantly effective in many ways. They can be a great way of managing anger.

One exercise involves breathing in a positive and/or breathing out a negative. It's a very simple thing to do. You need to find somewhere to sit comfortably and relax, and then focus on your breathing in and out, in and out, in and out. Keep doing that over and over again; you should find it calming, especially once you start to focus on it.

As you breathe in, imagine a positive emotion such as love filling your lungs and being sent out into every part of your body. Continue this exercise – breathing in love for as long as five minutes, or whatever's right for you.

This same exercise can be used to breathe out negative emotions – anger, most often. As you practise, you will find that you can often get into a rhythm where you breathe out a negative emotion such as resentment and breathe in a positive one: acceptance. Try it – it takes some getting used to as you've got to get your head round the idea but it works really well for many people.

Thursday 6 December 2012

I feel like I've been here for months. I am feeling down every day and it seems to be getting worse at the moment. We have ward round today, where we get our chance to speak to Dr Webster. Ward round is what I'm waiting for. It's the only hope of making progress or hearing when things might be happening. You then go back to the endless daily cycle.

Ward round happens once a week. It's on a Thursday and everyone is on edge because they know they could get called to Dr Webster's office at any time. It could be any time from early in the morning and up to times like 8pm.

* * *

I know I will get nervous when I see him and make inappropriate jokes about being thin, running away and killing myself. I'm like my dad at times, always making an awful joke at exactly the wrong moment. I only say these things because it's intimidating sitting in a room with everyone watching your every move.

It won't last long – five minutes. I am told by the staff to take in a list of notes or things I want to ask him, because, if not, I will forget to ask things I want to find out. I only have one question and that is easy to remember – 'When do I get out of this hellhole?'

* * *

I've just found out that I can't continue with my master's degree because I'm here. Niamh texted me saying she made the choice to call my university and say I'm not coming back. I feel everything is collapsing around me. It feels like my walls are caving in and things are getting worse. I'm told it's for the best but I can't see that right now. I'm starting to feel lost and beginning to lose hope. Christmas also feels like it's fading away. I don't have much to hold on to at the moment. I need something.

* * *

It's now almost 'snack time', which is where we all sit around like we are in some weird playgroup and eat snacks. We are watched hawk-eyed to make sure we don't throw food away or stuff it under cushions. I've already found chocolate bars stuffed down the sides of sofas and have seen people cramming food into their pockets. Some people here have awful OCD and prepping food takes ages. Others eat food in particular ways like cutting an orange in half and eating it with a fork. It's agony watching them. It must be hell for them.

* * *

I still haven't seen Dr Webster yet as, throughout the day, we are called one-by-one to see him randomly during activities. I think the activity today will be yoga. We have certain classes/activities on different days. It's a bit like being back at school but instead of Maths and English it's body image and let's not kill ourselves.

I think the waiting is designed to make us try to cope with the anxiety. The fact that the meeting could spring up at any point means you are constantly on edge. Having to deal with that is actually a lot harder than it sounds, but I think he knows that.

* * *

I just spoke to Dr Webster and have been told I'm staying here until after Christmas. I'm feeling at my lowest – just want to fade away. I have felt suicidal at times and right now it's very much at the front of my mind. Who wouldn't, though? I'm stuck in this place with no set time frame, and when I get out, if I do, it's back to the real world. That in itself is a scary prospect. Imagine having to tell people why you have been away for so many months. It's hard to not give up hope.

Now, to top things off, I have to go and have dinner with all the other crazy people whilst being treated like a child. This is where we get marched through locked corridors, get checked and then after the meal we have to sit and be watched for 45 minutes. Meal times are pretty awful to have to witness let alone be a part of. We sit around in a group whilst various staff members sit and watch our every move. We're given very specific amounts and allowances, even including salt and pepper. Most of the people in here have some sort of OCD rituals when it comes to eating. If you're not mental before this, you soon will be.

I hate it here. It drives me mad.

ANGER EXERCISE 3: THE JUNGLE PATHWAY

There is a visualisation technique that has worked well for many people who see a hugely difficult time ahead – for Michael, at this point, getting through another week locked up. You have to imagine you are faced, all around you, with a thick, dense jungle; trees and vines and creepers all block your way. There is no path at all and it's almost impossible to see a way through.

You sit on the ground and then focus on the jungle. Imagine a path opening up behind – *behind* – you. Try to see it in your mind's eye as clearly as you can. The trees and the vines and the creepers all pulling back to leave a pathway clear for you. Focus more and see that pathway opening up wider and wider.

You then stand and turn. You can see the wide-open pathway in front of you. Walk forward on to the path and feel yourself moving, striding now, along between all the trees as you move your way through. Some people find this works for them; it gives them a sense of self-belief and strength.

Friday 7 December 2012

Today I woke up and I feel awesome – ha, ha, not bloody likely. Once again, I'm about to be patrolled to breakfast where I'm watched eagle-eyed by the staff. There's a group of about ten of us, which can vary depending on whether someone's tried to leg it or is on a home visit. I'm followed to the coffee machine to watch how much sugar I put in my drink and how much milk I put on my Weetabix. I'm enjoying playing games to wind up the staff. I keep swapping food about as if I can't make my mind up and then pour my cereal and milk out as slowly as possible.

One girl here called Tia has a severe eating disorder and really bad OCD. This means she has to carry out ritualistic behaviour to feel safe. It gets to the point where she has to pour her cereal and milk in such a certain way that it's painful to watch.

Am I really that mental? I guess I must be to be here.

Maybe they watch me doing the same sort of thing? I've tried to think about any weird things I do, but really what is normal? We are told how to act and be from the day we are born. If you actually sit and think about some of the everyday things we do, it's pretty strange. Like people sitting round watching soaps on TV – pretend versions of life. We are living life and yet people still choose to watch fake stuff like that.

I know I'm weird and it's hard to actually say what I do that's weird. I just know I am and that's why I'm here. I have noticed I have OCD tendencies, like having to do my hair in a certain way or having to do things at the same time every day. I don't think I have bad OCD. I've been diagnosed with mild OCD, but it's linked to my other issues. I think it's again down to control. I know my mind and body are out of control so I have to have control over little things, like the way I brush my hair, that make me feel like I have some power.

Saturday 8 December 2012

Niamh is allowed to come and have dinner with me tonight. She isn't allowed to have dinner every night – it depends on how many times Dr Webster says she can come in a week. It's Sunday tomorrow and I'm allowed to go out in the car with Niamh for a drink somewhere nearby. We will be set a scheduled amount of time to go out. This could be my chance to make a getaway. I think we will get an hour to an hour and a half of time out, so it's not much but enough.

I still have to be weighed daily, which is horrible as I'm woken at 6am, have to strip down and stand in a freezing cold room in front of someone who carefully checks me. Before being weighed you have to go to the toilet and you're not allowed to drink – the staff think you're trying to drink a lot of water to increase your weight which would mean you get out of here that much faster.

For me, it's all a game. The aim is to keep my weight going up. If it does go up, I am one step closer to home; if it drops, it means my meal plan is increased. Even worse, the staff think I am skipping food, hiding it or vomiting it back up – none of which I have ever actually done.

This – the focus on getting weight up – is where I think the Priory and places like it can fail. I am very aware already that the aim is to hit a target weight, linked to BMI (body mass index), which is crazy in my opinion. I think there should be more of a focus on fixing the way people think. The weight is still very important, but without the right way of thinking nothing else matters. As it stands, as long as you're on their good side, you are more likely to get out – even if, in your head, you are still completely mental.

I'm now reading *The Hobbit* because there's not much else to do except stare at the ceiling. My antidepressants have been increased, which is never a good sign. I'm still taking citalopram – not sure of the dosage, I just know it's a lot. Every day feels harder to get through, and to be honest I'm feeling a lot of anger. I don't even really know what at. I think it's a mixture of my own stupidity, the environment I'm stuck in and the staff looking down on me. I'm feeling really low and I know that the staff are noticing it. I'm failing at 'the game' at the moment. I feel like my life is falling apart.

ANGER EXERCISE 4: LETTING GO OF THE PAST

Anger is a natural emotion but it can also be a destructive one, both internally on your mental health and externally on your relationship with others, if it does not subside. There are many anger management exercises you can try to help control these feelings. We have talked of one or two already, involving cane snapping and breathing. Here is another that we have come across over the years that might work for you. It's called 'letting go of the past'.

Sit somewhere quiet and peaceful and try to imagine yourself sitting alone in the middle of a huge cathedral or other old and sacred place appropriate to your beliefs. It could be a huge dark cave, as long as it is somewhere you can feel at ease.

Now bring your earliest memories into your mind and try to see them in your head as they happened. You now want to try to imagine letting them go into the dark, faraway corners of the cave. 'I release these memories. I have moved on. I am free.'

Now try to move on and visualise the moments in your life that have been turning points and changed your direction. Again, imagine letting these go away into the vastness of the cave. Again: 'I release these memories. I have moved on. I am free.'

Wherever you imagine you are sitting – a cave is probably a place that suits everyone regardless of beliefs – you should see this as representing your past where all of your memories go. They stay there whilst you move on with your life. They are always there if you want to revisit the good ones. The others can stay there, hidden far away in the shadows. Let them be. When you are ready, imagine yourself leaving the cave and moving on.

Sunday 9 December 2012

Last night, Niamh came here for dinner. She seemed exhausted and we are finding it hard to talk. I think it's starting to get very difficult between us. I can't blame her, though. Who wants a boyfriend in a nuthouse?

* * *

I was weighed this morning and my weight hasn't changed at all which means the food will be increased again. The body is a weird thing – the more you eat, the more your body starts to burn it off.

At mealtimes, you literally have to finish every bit of food off your plate – almost to the point where you have to lick every last crumb.

There have been points where people refuse to eat any more and we all sit there for well over an hour whilst the staff try to force that person to eat. It ends with the last person eating whilst tears roll down their cheeks.

* * *

My meal plan has increased. I think this is another flaw in the way it works here. More attention should be put into getting people's heads right rather than just fattening them up.

My issue is about feeling low rather than trying to be skinny. If I feel depressed, I don't feel like eating. So the focus, for me anyway, should be on the mood side really.

I'm starting to get panic attacks because I feel trapped. It's so claustrophobic being locked in here with minimal sunlight. Everybody always feels on edge and I have snapped at people a couple of times already.

* * *

I have been getting back into my drawing, which is good. I don't think I've sat down and drawn properly in a long time. My work has always been quite dark and being here is giving me plenty of inspiration.

I've been trying various breathing techniques which are designed to help calm me and lower my heart rate. If I'm feeling panicky, I take my focus away from the room, shut my eyes and breathe and focus on nothing but breathing.

* * *

This afternoon, Niamh came down again and we went out for an hour. We wandered around a few shops whilst people stared at me – and I really do mean stare because I look a mess. I know people look because I'm so thin, and I know it's not just me thinking it because Niamh tends to say something back if a stranger stares too much or makes a comment.

I can't begin to describe what it feels like to only go outside for an hour after being locked indoors for days on end. The only thing I can compare it to is like being a naughty child or being in prison. I'm an adult and I'm being told what to do at all times.

I have made a good friend here called Wilko. He is the only other man on my unit and he's in a pretty bad way. He can barely walk without holding on to the walls and he struggles really badly with eating anything. I saw he was upset a lot today so I went into his room, which is not allowed, and we chatted a while. He has had a pretty horrific past with some awful things that have happened to him in his life.

* * *

Tonight, my mum and dad are coming to see me which is making me nervous. Niamh has always seen me like this every day for ages, but I don't like my family to see me a mess and so thin, probably because I'm ashamed and the people here are all clearly mental. There are people who can barely walk and I know the addicts are literally in the next corridor.

I don't know what my parents will make of all of this. I imagine they will be scared and shocked by the whole thing. There are drug and sex addicts, depressed people and people with all sorts of other problems I can't even begin to explain. You can often hear swearing, shouting and people screaming. It's like *One Flew Over the Cuckoo's Nest*. It's a madhouse.

I really want to see my younger brother, Adam, but I don't think my parents will bring him tonight because of the people here and the way I look.

OUR VISIT TO THE PRIORY

One of the things to consider when reading Michael's diary is that, however sane he might sound at times, he was in the Priory partly because of his anorexia but mostly because of his mental ill-health. That's worth remembering, I think. He wasn't 100 per cent clear and straight in his mind. How could he possibly be after everything that had happened to him?

Depression, anxiety and other issues can all be seen reflected in what Michael writes, but there are also moments where it is plain that he is not thinking properly about the help he was getting – with talk of all this being a game and a sense that the doctors and staff are toying with him at times and, almost but not quite, out to get him.

I guess that's not surprising – he was mentally ill and his physical health was not good either, of course. Anorexia, and its effect on the body including blood vessels, can have a damaging effect on the workings of the brain, decision making, etc. In simple terms, anorexics don't always 'think straight'. It would be too much to expect that they could.

I'll come later to my own interactions with Dr Webster – a good guy for sure – but, first, let's look at our visit to see Michael in the Priory, 'to compare notes', as it were, on what it was like there. Tracey and I had wanted to visit Michael for a while, but Niamh seemed to visit every night – rattling down the A12 and back, a 100-or-so-mile round trip, in a clapped-out old banger – so we had to wait our turn. Niamh's mother appeared to be a regular visitor too. It bothered us quite a lot that we were some way back in the queue but we kept quiet about it rather than risk a falling-out. We did not take Adam with us; we wanted to protect him from what we expected to see. And Sophie was up at Durham doing her degree.

Going into the Priory was daunting and scary; we did not know what to expect. Pulling up in the car park, the building looked like a big old Travelodge. It was quiet. The car park was fairly empty. We walked to the entrance, neither of us speaking, both of us nervous. As often happens when confronted with a locked door and a bell and various buttons, I tend to press all of them in turn repeatedly and hope something happens soon.

Eventually, a no-nonsense female member of staff – a nurse in manner – opened the door and, after introductions and bag checks, led us through a maze of corridors and security systems. She seemed pleasant enough, although I would not have wanted to arm-wrestle her.

We entered reception and we were struck by the number of young girls – all elbows, knees and sunken eyes – sitting awkwardly in a semi-circle of chairs. We waited for a moment or two – I think we were being signed in – not knowing where to look. My default reaction when faced with something out of my comfort zone is to make a joke, usually out of place and with those around me stunned into silence.

There were no jokes tonight. It was all too awful to see – these anorexic girls just sitting there like zombies. We hurried through, along a neat and tidy corridor, to Michael's anonymous room. We were shown in and, other than a nurse putting his head round the door once or twice, were left alone for the next half hour or so.

It looked like a nice and clean budget-hotel room: a simple bed, a chair, shelf, TV, mirror, en-suite bathroom – and Michael, stick boy himself, sitting up in bed. Tracey hugged him. She's quite good at that sort of thing. I couldn't really look at him. Struggling with my emotions, I turned away and looked instead at Michael's bits and pieces on the side, straightening them, fiddling about, moving to the wash basin, composing myself as best I could. If I'd had a duster and polish, I would have had more of a tidy. Anything to avoid facing this. Aware that if I spoke now, my heartbreak emotions would be heard in my voice.

We settled and then talked, albeit fairly superficially, as if we were visiting someone in hospital who had had some sort of embarrassing operation – what my mother would have mouthed 'down there'. I felt awkward, not sure what to say. This was not the moment for questions and explanations and recriminations and apologies; I knew that. We needed to keep it light and pleasant.

Michael looked thin and tired but he talked comfortably enough with us. We talked as normally as we could: of what was happening at home, with Sophie and with Adam, and then what Michael was doing, whether he was watching anything on the television, whether he needed anything; underwear and socks formed the basis of a lengthy conversation with

Tracey. I had an equally long conversation about buying him a DVD or two that he could watch to keep himself busy. *Dexter* seemed to be one series he liked and Michael had seen this season and not that season and half of another one, so I said I would get him one or two he had not seen. And I did.

And then we left, Tracey hugging him again, me avoiding all that sort of stuff with a 'Look after yourself, see you soon.' We made our way out, shown to the door by the same member of staff who brought us in and took us through to Michael. For us, the place seemed quiet and organised, and the staff we saw and spoke to seemed friendly and professional. Other than the young girls at reception and the fact that we were checked in and out carefully, we would not have been aware what this place actually was. Michael, being there all the time, would have seen another side.

I cried – that it had all come to this, our son locked away – in the car on the way home. Then we stopped at Burger King and ate burgers and drank Cokes in the car park. We felt relief that Michael was where he was and thought it was the best place for him. The meeting went okay and I think we all felt better for it.

Monday 10 December 2012

Last night, my mum and dad came up to see me. I think they were pleased to have a chance to come in, but I could see they were both really upset by it all. I think they were also a little nervous to be in this sort of environment.

* * *

Today was an interesting day. We were at breakfast when the staff suddenly noticed that Liv was missing. Members of staff were panicking and I could see that something could kick off. You never really see the staff flustered and today I could see panic on their faces.

I looked out of the window from the food hall and saw Liv legging it down the front driveway in her pyjamas pursued by two women running at full speed. I presume they caught her because I saw her sitting in the communal area later in the day.

* * *

I would like to run. I think I probably could get out. But I don't know where I'd go. I can't run all the way back up the A12 to home. They'd catch me. It would make things worse if that were possible. I'd be here longer anyway.

Tuesday 11 December 2012

Last night, I saw Niamh and her mum. That went okay, but sometimes it can get too much talking about all of this all of the time. People always want to talk to try to make sense of it and to help in some way. But none of it really makes sense and I don't want to talk about it anyway.

* * *

Making choices is a really big issue for me. It always has been and the last few years have been a nightmare. It's all linked to anxiety. Anxiety plays with your head and makes it very difficult to come to a rational decision. Having severe anxiety makes it very hard to commit to something, and even the daily meal choices are testing. It would take a normal person probably seconds to decide what to have; it can take me as long as an hour.

Everything here seems to be a test. I think they are seeing what makes us tick – once again, it's clear to me that we are playing a game. I often feel like I'm in *Big Brother* or some kind of reality TV show. I always thought the people on those TV shows were crazy, but us lot in here are straight-up mental. Like people not being able to pour milk on to their cereal without crying about it.

* * *

I've just had scrambled eggs on toast and then went to yoga. I feel like some sort of hipster but I feel relaxed about it.

Wednesday 12 December 2012

I've just been told I have something called a CPA (care plan assessment) meeting on the third of January which is a much more serious version of ward round, where they discuss how I'm doing and what sort of mental state I'm in. They give you a chance to talk briefly, but it will probably be them talking at me. It's like the bonus round in this weird game and the aim is to act normal in front of them all. If I don't say anything too mental or start crying, that will be a big help.

* * *

Today, we had a group trip out. Basically, the people who are thought to be doing okay get to go out for the morning on a walk about town together – it must look like some kind of freak show. Wilko doesn't do well as he has social anxiety. This basically means he doesn't like being around people, especially strangers in a public place. It's something I struggle with too, although my issues are less extreme than Wilko's. I don't think anyone would know I was struggling, but it's obvious with Wilko.

He had a really bad panic attack and I didn't know what to do and, to be honest, it was pretty scary to watch. He basically either starts to hyperventilate, get angry or go into shock. If this happens, we have to try to help him breathe, or if it gets too bad, we all just have to leave wherever we are. Getting out and about is good practice for him, though.

* * *

Niamh came for dinner this evening. I had bought her some presents from my trip out. I didn't get much – just a candle and flowers. She always tells me that I need to treat myself as I don't know how to be good to myself. I don't think I've got anything in months. I think it's again to do with me punishing myself as I feel guilty for being this way and I have no self-worth, so why would I look after myself?

I'm trying to get to sleep but am feeling anxious. Quite a few things are troubling me. Tomorrow, we are having our Christmas lunch which I'm feeling anxious about. I don't like eating in front of people. Wilko and others have said I'm looking better, which basically means bigger. I don't want to be bigger, i.e. fatter. I have ward round tomorrow, so I will hopefully find out what's happening at the weekend. I am worried about that a lot.

ANXIETY EXERCISE 1: THE BLACK BIRDS

Michael ended up in hospital and went into the Priory essentially because he was anorexic – his weight loss had led to his body closing down on him. The hospital patched him up physically and the Priory was there to help him mentally, and to help him put on weight too.

The thing with mental illness – and I'm no expert but this is how it seems to me – is that it is rarely a simple, straightforward thing; it never seems to be one, single issue. If only it were 'just' anxiety or 'just' OCD (awful though these are in themselves). It never seems to be. Michael, like many other sufferers, had a multitude of issues, one leading to another, some overlapping, doubling back, twisting into each other, making all of them worse. Imagine an octopus-type monster with lots of tentacles, some still, other writhing. That is the intertwined, tangled, suffocating nature of mental illness that many people experience.

The heavy-duty issues really started with what might be called low-level issues, primarily anxiety. Left unchecked, as it was with Michael, this can be debilitating. The reality, of course, is that there are really no low-level issues as they are all awful for the sufferer, but we are obviously trying to untangle and separate issues into awful, really awful, life-threatening awful and so on, to try to make some sort of sense of what is often senseless.

We will look at several anxiety-related exercises as we move into the book. But Michael has written of anxiety and not wanting to be near people several times now – an example of one issue rolling into another and then back again to make matters worse. Michael felt anxious. He did not want to be with people. Knowing he had to be made him more anxious. The anxiety levels went up when he was with people, so he wanted to be with them less. Endless – around and around he went, down and down.

Let's start looking at anxiety – as Michael has mentioned anxiety stopping him from sleeping – with an exercise to aid sleep. Sit or lie down somewhere that's peaceful and comfortable, and close your eyes.

Now focus on your breath, listening to yourself breathing in and out and in and out, slowly and steadily. In and out. In and out. Slowly. Steadily. Tune in to your breathing until that is your only focus. In and out. In and out. Slowly. Steadily. This in itself should help you to start to relax and is something you can build into your day on an 'as needed' basis. Slow breathing is a brilliant way to reclaim some calm.

Now, imagine a flock of black birds circling just above your head. They're not going to touch you or harm you or anything like that. You're safe. One hundred per cent. They just want your attention. You can imagine them flying around you, calling out, occasionally swooping closer to make you look at them. These black birds represent whatever it is that's making you feel anxious.

The next time one swoops close, reach out in your imagination and catch it ever so gently. You don't want to hurt it, just hold it in your hand. Feel how light and inconsequential it really is. It's just a small, squawky, noisy bird – that's all. There is no weight or substance to it. Let it go! Throw it ever so gently skywards. Watch it fly away until it is just a dot in the distance.

Now catch the next bird and the next, repeating this 'catch and let go' process time and time again until all you can see are these little black dots far, far away. You should feel a sense of relief as you release each bird and a sense of peace when they have all flown away from you. All done? Time to sleep…

Thursday 13 December 2012

Today, there is ward round which means everyone will be on edge and ready to snap. Let's practise being normal. On the inside, I'm screaming 'Let me out.'

* * *

I think that there's a chance I might get to go home for a night at the weekend which would be my first step to getting out of this hellhole.

Others who have been here longer than me come and go a lot more because they have made progress (i.e. they play the game).

* * *

I started the day as usual by being weighed. It turns out I'm 46.8 kilos. I feel like I've been stuffing myself now for days on end. My weight is increasing and that feels weird. I don't like not being in control.

I've just had my breakfast and am getting ready for another day in paradise.

Today I have the Christmas lunch – this will be a test.

I think I will go back to my room afterwards, put on a DVD and try not to think about how crap this all is.

I hate having to sit with everyone. I know people will look at me. They will pretend to not be watching my every move, but I'm not stupid and know they will watch. I'd be the same.

I don't like the atmosphere, and being with others who are mental makes me realise just how crazy I am.

It can be a laugh, though, at times. Well, not really a laugh to a normal person. To a normal person it's probably quite concerning.

* * *

I get to go home for one night at the weekend!

Anxiety exercise 2: Breathing
through alternate nostrils

Taking control of your breathing patterns can be effective at all sorts of times when you're not feeling so good. When you're stressed, for example, your breathing can become fast and irregular and that can have a knock-on effect on your physical health, blood pressure, etc. The key is to be aware of this and, when it happens, to take charge by breathing in and out deeply and slowly.

Try taking a long, deep breath, holding it and then breathing slowly out until you feel you have emptied all the air from your lungs. You can do this three or four times, one after the other, each time trying to focus solely on your breathing. Some people find it helpful to imagine they are breathing in whatever is making them feel anxious and then blowing it all away as they breathe out.

Michael only dabbled a little with yoga – it's not something he's done long-term – but one exercise there helped him. It involved breathing deeply through alternate nostrils. It's really simple. Close your left nostril and breathe in slowly through the right. Breathe in as deeply as you can. Next, close both nostrils and hold your breath whilst counting slowly to 20. Release the left nostril, keeping the right one closed. Breathe out as long and as slowly as you can until you've emptied it all out. Repeat the exercise with the right nostril and alternate up to ten times or so, until you feel calm.

Friday 14 December 2012

I woke up feeling drained. At least I'm starting to recognise I wake up depressed every day. I can sort of separate myself from it in a way. One day I hope I can wake up again in my own bed without being yelled at by a horrible member of staff. This tends to happen when they come to do the early-morning weigh-in and I don't make things easy for them. By this I mean I simply don't get up until they physically pull the covers off me and turn the lights on.

Today, I'm seeing Richard and I hope he helps settle my mind. Richard seems to connect with me more than anyone I've spoken to. I think it simply comes down to the fact that he understands mental health, but more importantly he talks to me like a friend. He doesn't look down on me or judge me at all. He simply suggests theories, ideas and positive outlooks on situations.

* * *

We talked about 'decatastrophising'. This is basically where you try to see things differently and attempt to stop catastrophic ways of thinking.

This can happen when you overthink a situation in a negative way, think about how awful it's going to be and therefore panic about an event.

Decatastrophising is a way of thinking to over-come negative thoughts attached to upcoming events.

Often, the event is never as bad as you might expect, so Richard might ask me to talk about similar events in my past and how I feel about them now. It sort of helps put things in perspective. It was okay before, so it will be okay next time.

* * *

Richard was really helpful and tried to help me see things from a different perspective. He talks about what life could be like for me and also tries to reinforce that it's not too late for me to have a good life. I just need to keep my head down and get on with it, but that's really hard when all I want is for the ground to swallow me up.

Niamh isn't coming over tonight because she's got work stuff on, so that's a real blow. It means I have nothing to look forward to at all today. It makes me feel even more empty as there is very little purpose to the day. I have to have something that keeps me going, otherwise it becomes a big struggle.

* * *

Tomorrow, I get to go home for the night. I thought I would be pleased but I'm actually very nervous about it. I feel there is a lot of pressure on me and Niamh to make sure it all goes well and that I get back on time. They judge if it went well by my weight, what I did with my time and how they perceive me to be feeling.

I feel like I have been locked in this hellhole for ever. The initial thought that I'd be in here for two weeks or so is clearly not the case. I was told I'd be here a couple of weeks by my mental health team at the hospital. I feel I've wasted so much of my life already and this process just feels like an ongoing nightmare.

* * *

I just spoke to Chris the dietitian about the weekend. Chris basically has the weigh-in details and then decides on a suitable meal plan that will increase my weight. It's all pretty straightforward. If my weight's not going up, the food piles up.

It's a weird feeling being scared to go outside into the real world. I remember a similar feeling when I was discharged from hospital after almost dying. I felt very scared because I thought I was going to die. I remember getting home and my legs being so messed up I couldn't walk properly and literally had to drag myself up the stairs by the banister.

I feel like I don't have a home any more. I have been in and out of hospital, I can't really remember much of what has happened to me and now I'm here. My head doesn't feel settled.

* * *

I haven't heard from anyone today, not even Niamh. I get odd letters and emails from my dad about stuff that makes him laugh, but I've not heard from him either for a day or two. I feel so isolated here when I'm just sitting for hours on end in my room.

I need to find a way to learn how to be happy and why I don't allow myself to see the good things in life. I always feel the need to punish and hate myself.

I think the medication has started to make me numb and to feel a little more dead inside.

I feel like I've let everyone down and I'm a huge disappointment. I should really be happy but I'm not. I think that's why I punish myself. I have no self-worth and don't feel like I deserve to have a life when I've hurt people so much.

ANXIETY EXERCISE 3: THE BLUE BUBBLE

Many of Michael's issues revolved around difficulties with other people – watching him eat, seeing him in the street and engaging with him in social situations. 'The blue bubble' is a technique that is often suggested, in varying forms, by experts trying to help those with anxiety and, more specifically, social anxiety. It can be effective when you have to be in a crowded room or on a packed-out bus or train, or even in the street.

It's really, really simple. You visualise a blue bubble around your body, protecting you (blue is widely regarded as a colour associated with peace and protection). As you move about, this blue bubble protects you from those around you. As an alternative, you can imagine drawing a circle around yourself on the ground. As you move around, this protective circle moves with you, its invisible walls protecting you from top to toe. It's something that can work well once you have the idea in your head.

Saturday 15 December 2012

Today, I'm going home for the night which is both exciting and scary. Niamh will be coming soon to pick me up. I feel like I hate myself and don't want anyone to see me. I feel ashamed.

In some ways, I think being at home is going to make me sadder because I'm going to see what I'm missing out on.

If and when I do eventually get out of this place, I need to make sure it's for good – I'm not coming back to this hell.

Sunday 16 December 2012

Yesterday, I got to go home for the day and night. On the way back, we stopped at the big Tesco at Copdock. It seemed so busy and hectic with everyone hurrying about and no one standing still. I can't even describe how weird it feels to walk about in public after being locked away. Imagine having every simple privilege taken away from you. Like being able to open a window or go to the toilet without being checked on.

We then went into town and I did my best to keep my head down and hope no one I know saw me. We didn't really do anything in town apart from go for a drink and have a wander round the shops. I didn't buy anything.

I'm reading a book called *Crank*, which is really bizarre but very interesting. It's so blunt and has the text all over the place to show the character is going crazy. My diary should look like that.

I'm having to get in the right frame of mind for another long, horrible week of being watched. I don't really even know how to think positively about being here. It feels like an endless nightmare. The only thing that gives me hope is getting out, but I literally have no idea when that could be. I think it will be months rather than weeks and that makes me sad.

POSITIVITY EXERCISE 1:
TURNING NEGATIVES POSITIVE

Many of Michael's troubles come from issues of anxiety and being negative and assuming the worst will happen. There is an exercise – and you'll see versions of it in many self-help books – that involves replacing negative thoughts with positive ones, and it can work well if you are not too far down the path or have come out the other side and want to keep on top of things. This exercise is similar to those used in Michael's CBT sessions.

For example, 'I never know what to say in a conversation' – something many of us worry about – can become 'But I can listen to what the other person says and ask them something about that'. Experts will suggest all sorts of activities that can also help from carrying cards with positive statements to putting 10p in a jar for every positive thought and 10p in another jar for every negative thought and, as you focus on turning negatives into positives, seeing how the positive jar piles up with coins. You may start with more coins in your negative jar but that should change over time as you think more positively.

All good in their way – but we think the place to start is by being aware of negative thoughts and then monitoring them in the first place. We all know someone who sees the downside in everything. Often, they do not realise it – at best, when pressed, they see themselves as 'honest' or 'realistic' or 'plain-speaking'. Those around them see them as a misery guts.

Many people don't realise how negative the mind can be and how downbeat thoughts can swarm over everything. There have been times when I have said to Michael, 'If you won five million pounds on the lottery, you'd find the negatives in that' (and, to be fair, there are times when he would have done). It's a matter of trying to see the upsides and focusing on them.

Here's a simple little exercise that you may find useful. List, let's say, 30 negative things about yourself (it doesn't have to be bang on 30 – do what feels about right). Write each of these out, one at a time, on 30 postcards. Then try to write 30 matching but positive statements on another 30 postcards. Pair them up, one negative with its corresponding positive. For example, 'I'm quite shy and can never begin a conversation' may be a negative. 'I can smile at someone and they may start a conversation' may be a positive. Every day, take one pair and focus on repeating the positive statement at regular intervals through the day.

Monday 17 December 2012

I came back to the Priory last night and Niamh stayed and had dinner with me, which was nice. We then went back to my room and I pretty much passed out. It's not long until Christmas now and it feels horrendous being locked up here. I still have no idea at all when I will be discharged.

I was weighed this morning and I have increased to 47.5 kilos. Weight going up always looks good when it comes to ward round.

Time is always passing, which means I'm closer to leaving, as long as I don't go mental...well, even more mental.

I have now kind of given up on Christmas this year and realise it's not going to happen. I haven't got Niamh or my family any presents so I'm feeling pretty awful about that.

I have been called to see the big man (Dr Webster) and that's making me very nervous. I might ask him if I can go home during the week to try being on my own for a while when Niamh is at work. It's worth a try.

I'm starting to hate looking in the mirror – I hate myself so much. I hate who I am, from the way I look to the way I think. I do feel stronger and have more energy, but getting bigger very quickly is hard. I'm going to watch *Where the Wild Things Are* in bed and do nothing.

* * *

This afternoon I saw Dr Webster. He was pleased with how I did at the weekend. My weight had gone up and that's really all they look for. I will see him again on Thursday. I think there might be a chance I get two nights at home next weekend. It's getting very close to Christmas now and I still don't know what's happening. He always seems to be planning my next step – whether it's good or bad news. I don't feel I have any control over things.

Dr Webster keeps stressing that I need to be careful and repeating that I could have easily died. He says I'm one of the few people he's met who has come so close to dying. Part of me thinks he's trying to scare me into getting better. Another part of me is starting to think that his plan is to keep me here a lot longer.

Tuesday 18 December 2012

I only just woke up in time for breakfast so I had to throw on my clothes fast and join the other weirdos. There was a massive fuss at breakfast today because Becky refused to eat, which means we all sit around waiting whilst staff try to persuade her. She also has severe OCD and finds it difficult to even pour her milk. Being here has made me realise people suffer in such different ways. Whether it's having OCD or a fear of leaving their homes.

It makes me think about how and why people get into these habits or ways of thinking. Some of it is genetic but some of it comes down to habit, addiction or simply not thinking straight.

I have CBT soon with Richard, and yoga if I can face embarrassing myself. I feel ugly and want a haircut. It helps a bit.

* * *

Tomorrow, I'm out with the rehab group again. It's where we get to go into town. I'm now allowed to buy my own lunch in town and then bring it back here. I'll probably go to M&S and get something. It's all pretty humiliating as we are watched by staff in a public place.

Going out in the group is very embarrassing. Partly because, as a group, we are all clearly barking mad one way or the other, whether it's Wilko going into a fit or Tia crying her eyes out, but also because, as we shuffle around the shops, the staff from the Priory keep a watchful eye on us. It makes me feel even more mental or some sort of criminal. I might pretend to leg it for a laugh.

* * *

I just had my CBT session, where we talked about why I'm a lunatic and act the way I do. Richard also met Niamh and we all got to talk. I think that helped me and Niamh understand each other a bit more and it also gave Richard a chance to see us together.

Wednesday 19 December 2012

I now hate how I look in the mirror. I feel like crap. I feel fat. I know I'm not fat, but in comparison with what I was I'm massive. I have always felt ugly and hated how I look. I can't really change that, though. I don't know how I wish I'd look; I think it's more a case that I'm not comfortable in my skin.

* * *

Today is the rehab group trip. Time to parade about with the others with the public staring at us as if we are freaks in a circus.

Niamh should be coming up tonight to see me.

Time is passing so slowly. I spoke to Petra today and she has been here almost a whole year. I can't bear the thought of being here that length of time, but I have to come to terms with the fact that it might happen. I get to speak to Dr Webster soon and find out about Christmas. I have given up on it, though.

* * *

I've just got back from the rehab trip. It was actually pretty cool. I got to have a chat with Richard and to walk on our own for a bit. We just talked about everyday things for a change. He was probably just trying to see what I was like in a relatively normal situation and was testing me, but I like to think he likes me and we are mates. I had some blood tests the other day and have been told it's all looking a lot better – well, at least I'm not dying any more, so that's something, isn't it?

* * *

We had lunch at the lodge, a small building separate from the other patients, for a change. The better you do, the nicer things you get to do. If you eat meals properly, your weight increases and you engage with staff positively, then you're winning the game.

* * *

This afternoon, I had a body image session with Paula who always makes me laugh. This class is about trying to recognise what it is we don't like about ourselves and how we can learn to cope with that or possibly change how we see ourselves. I got pretty upset when we spoke about my past. Having to go over bad stuff that happened is always very draining and I don't really like having to talk about it.

What I don't like about myself!

I feel ugly and have felt so for a long time. I don't know why – I just don't like how I look.

I also feel uncomfortable because I'm getting bigger, my clothes are tighter and I feel bloated.

I also don't like that I'm shy and quiet.

I don't like being around people.

I just don't like people – ha!

I probably don't cope with these things in a very good way. I just push it all deep down inside, which makes me feel worse. I try to be around people, but at the moment I just don't like it. Maybe in the future I will feel more confident.

* * *

Becky said I still look underweight and like a skeleton. I don't believe her. It's not that I think I'm fat; I just don't feel comfortable. I'm now just waiting for Niamh to arrive.

POSITIVITY EXERCISE 2: THOUGHT STOPPING

There are various ways you can try to stop negative thoughts and, as suggested, positive self-talk is one of them. There is a technique we have come across called thought stopping which may be effective on its own or alongside positive self-talk to emphasise it.

What you do is this. Find somewhere quiet and peaceful where you can relax a little (we'll come to some relaxation exercises soon enough). What you then do is bring that most troubling thought into your mind. Try to think it 'out loud' in your head – 'I have no self-confidence', for example.

Stop! Either think 'Stop!' or visualise a big red-and-black stop sign. Some experts will say you can actually say or shout 'Stop!' out loud. Whenever you find yourself thinking this, or any other negative thought, you can say 'Stop!' or, when that's not appropriate – if you're with people, for example – you can imagine that stop sign. Then try to replace that thought with something more positive.

Thursday 20 December 2012

My weight has dropped to 47.3 kilos. This could mean that I'm not going to get leave. It also means my meal plan will be increasing again. I'm just going to have to be open to whatever happens next. I feel gutted.

I hate Thursdays because of the early weigh-ins. Thursday is when we all get pulled out of bed at half five because that is when your weight is most accurate, apparently. I really can't relax and I want to see Chris the dietitian now. I feel like I'm getting frustrated with having to wait around to see people.

I think I might sneak into Wilko's room to play PlayStation games. It feels weird, two grown men having to sneak about to play games. We have only done it a couple of times, but it's cool getting to hang out because it makes things seem a little bit more normal.

Because my weight has dropped, I feel like I've taken a massive step backwards. This definitely means I will be staying here longer. I'm crying now because I feel like I'm going to be stuck here for ever and it just feels like a prison to me. I have just realised I have absolutely no say in anything that happens to me any more.

* * *

I've just seen the doctor. My meal plan has been increased because they think I have been making cutbacks somewhere without telling them, which I haven't. Weight is a weird thing, especially when your diet changes. Sometimes if you eat more, your body starts to have an increased metabolism, meaning you burn more calories. This process is taking so long and I'm beginning to realise the fastest way out is to eat my way out, which isn't really the best idea. You can be fat and mental, and that's okay. Thin, and whatever your mental state, that's not okay.

Me and Niamh argued today, I think because she's frustrated with this whole situation.

I have been thinking a lot about things. Mainly about what people have said to me. I think I hate myself and have for a long time. I don't know how to be kind to myself any more. Every day is about punishing myself.

Friday 21 December 2012

Today I get to go home for a while. Niamh's mum will be picking me up at 2pm and we will head back to Ipswich. She offered to pick me up because Niamh is at work and her mum has the day off and wanted to see me. I get two nights at home, but before I go I have to talk to the dietitian and then to Richard about things when I get back. He will just go over what I did whilst I went away and talk about my progress. I can talk most openly with Richard.

When you go on leave, you have your bags checked and you have to have a risk assessment. In the risk assessment, you get asked questions like these, in so many words:

How's your mood?

What are you going to get up to?

Do you feel like running away?

Are you going to kill yourself?

I always say, for the last one, 'I don't know; I'll see where the weekend takes me.' They never look impressed by my joke. It makes me smile, though.

The risk assessment seems pointless to me because I wouldn't tell them if I was planning to kill myself. If I was going to do it, I would have already done it by now.

Sunday 23 December 2012

I'm back in the Priory now after some time at home. I went into town with Niamh's mum the other day, which was nice. We went for a drink and I bumped into a friend I had not seen for a long time and we spoke for a few minutes and that seemed okay. I finally went to see *The Hobbit* with Niamh and geek out. It's weird how being locked up makes you really appreciate the smallest things in life. We take life for granted and it's only when things get really bad that you get to enjoy life.

It's back to reality, though, and I'm getting weighed very early in the morning before another day in hell. I hope I get to speak to Wilko soon. I know he has been struggling and I hope he's okay.

People take so much for granted and you only realise this when it's taken away. You don't really ever think about how you have the freedom to walk down the street, go to the shop or see your mates. I do now that I'm locked away.

* * *

I'm crying again.

It's good, though.

I've just been told I can go home for Christmas!

TALKING TO DR WEBSTER

We saw Michael once in the Priory in mid-December and since then had kept in touch with the odd silly but encouraging letter from me, parcels from Tracey and emails and texts, mostly from Sophie and Adam. As someone who has been used to organising and scheduling for much of my life, and never having had huge reserves of patience, I grew increasingly frustrated that Michael did not seem to know what was happening to him and when. It was all rather vague.

At this time, still not understanding mental health issues, I wanted to know what was being done to make him better and when he would be coming out. We wanted him to stay as long as he needed to, but were looking for some sort of timetable. (I know now, of course, that you cannot straighten and tidy and pack away and box off mental illness quite so neatly and to try to do so is generally pretty daft.)

Michael and I emailed each other about this and he seemed to want to know more too. He gave Dr Webster permission to talk to me. Although this seemed to take time to arrange – Michael did not see Dr Webster that often – it did mean I could put my concerns to Dr Webster and get some feedback from him. I could then talk to Michael about what was happening, which seemed to be what he wanted too.

For a long time, Tracey and I had had something of an issue with Niamh, although we tried our best to keep our concerns from her and Michael in case things blew up between us. Frankly, we thought this might be all her fault. When we had first met her, she was a slightly chubby girl but she had soon slimmed down. We thought for a while that Michael had followed her in dieting and had taken matters to an extreme. We also felt that Niamh was protecting and shielding Michael from us and that we were being kept at arm's length (which, to be fair, we were, albeit with the best intentions).

Then again, she had always been cheerful and jolly with us, at least early on; as Michael descended into his hell between 2010 and 2012, things did become increasingly strained. I recall Michael and Niamh – Niamh mostly, I think – not wanting to come on holiday to Spain with us in 2011 because of some sharp words I had said to them. And, a little later, I remember being in Ipswich town centre with them and the atmosphere being so strained that we barely spoke to each other.

We did not really know if Niamh was a good influence or a bad one on Michael, and so my first contact with Dr Webster was by email and, in essence, it was:

> Niamh has, in our view, exerted total control over Michael over the past five years and we are not sure that this is beneficial for Michael. Everything seems to suggest that he needs to get Niamh's agreement to do anything. It may be that we have misjudged Niamh. It may be that, without her, Michael would not even have got this far. Positive or negative, we cannot help but feel she is a key factor in all of this and, as such, would ask you to give this your consideration.

Dr Webster's reply was, as you'd expect, fairly non-committal, thanking me for the email and stating he would factor this into his work with Michael. Later, I spoke to Dr Webster on the telephone and he explained how close Michael had come to death and he talked a little of what they were doing with him. This seemed to be a mix of feeding him up to get his weight into the 'normal' BMI range and working on his mental health through a range of programmes; CBT, body image, etc. All good sensible stuff, really. He did not seem to think that Niamh was at fault at all, but indicated that they were 'too close' – that is, Michael was over-dependent on her which, with the benefit of hindsight, was the issue that we had misinterpreted.

The doctor's main concern seemed to be getting the balance right between keeping Michael there and letting him out for so many days and nights. Michael did not want to be there. He wanted to go. Dr Webster was worried that if he did not let him go home now and then, Michael would become difficult and uncooperative. If he did let him go, he thought that Michael may not come back and they'd have to move to get him sectioned. I got the impression that they'd cut Michael as much slack as they could, but that they were worried about him.

We felt reassured by the conversation and relayed the gist of it back to Michael: that he was doing well and was on course to get some leave. We did not mention the doctor's dilemma about Michael's leave from the Priory. We felt suggestions that Michael wasn't trusted 100 per cent and talk of not coming back and confrontations and being sectioned would possibly be something of a setback to him. I think anyone in that situation wants to hear 'You're doing well' rather than 'They don't trust you to come back...you might get sectioned.' We got that right: something of a first.

Monday 24 December 2012

I don't really know how I feel about Christmas. Part of me just wants it to be over, but I feel like I should at least try to enjoy it.

I really didn't sleep well last night. I think I've just got a lot on my mind. I was weighed early this morning and have gone from 47.3 to 48.0 kilos, which is very good news because it gives me a better chance of going home.

I can't describe how I'm feeling right now. I'm just not comfortable. I can't believe it's Christmas Eve today – it just doesn't seem like it. I feel really sad because I would normally do family stuff today including a panto in the morning and a cinema visit this afternoon. I miss the family Christmas routine.

When I was last out with Niamh, we went to the cinema to see *The Hobbit*. I saw my sister (Sophie) in the foyer and she burst into tears. She gave me a big hug – I've never seen her so upset.

Niamh wants to go to her sister and her sister's boyfriend's on Christmas day, which is fine, but I would have liked to have seen my own family at some point whilst I am out. I don't feel like being around other people who know I'm out of the loony bin for a short time.

I'm currently waiting to see Chris the dietitian. Seeing Chris is a scheduled thing which happens once a week. It's just about looking at what meal plan I am on and what changes need to be made.

I've just heard I'm going to have to move rooms which I'm annoyed about. Wilko only has a shower instead of a bath and keeps slipping over for some reason, so I'm swapping with him. It's annoying because I'm used to my room, but I don't mind swapping for Wilko.

THE MAITLAND CHRISTMAS

The Maitland Christmas is, I guess, like many families' Christmas, something of a well-established routine. We – usually seven or eight of us, what with assorted boyfriends and girlfriends – all go along and see the panto at the New Wolsey Theatre on Christmas Eve morning (they're brilliant!). We then all dash off to have lunch and get last-minute gifts and wrapping paper and sprouts and carrots and stuff. Tracey usually goes home to wrap things and talk to friends on the phone and drink. The rest of us go the cinema; this year, it was *Life of Pi*. In the evening, we usually have pizza and watch television.

None of us quite knew what Michael was doing on Christmas Eve, and whether he would suddenly appear at the pantomime or the film. Sophie had received a text to say he was coming out, so we knew he would be about. I think we all hoped he would appear out of the blue. He didn't, but we kept quiet rather than contact him or Niamh and maybe cause a rift. We wanted him to do whatever he wanted to do, whatever made him most happy.

Our Christmas Day is much the same as many other people's, I imagine. Bernard the dog usually gets a good walk first thing. We then tend to watch a DVD, something like *The Day After Tomorrow*. We have a huge Christmas dinner that no one can ever quite manage and a range of puddings; Tracey and I like a Christmas pudding with an orange in the middle. The children prefer chocolatey things. We do home-made crackers too with scratchcards in them and Sophie and Michael usually win something. We then open the presents, walk the dog again and watch (and nod off through) the *Doctor Who* Christmas special before we all slump at varying angles until it's time for bed.

There were some text messages between Michael and Tracey and Sophie and Adam on Christmas Day; we knew he was out and all was well, and that the presents we'd left in their shed on Christmas Eve had been received. Again, I think we hoped Michael would turn up at some point but probably wouldn't. He didn't.

In recent years, Boxing Days have been a bit less family-orientated, with football matches, early-starting New Year sales and trips to New York for Sophie and her boyfriend shortening the family festivities. Back in 2012, we still did much as we'd always done: walks, DVDs, games, a spread of cold meats and vegetables at tea-time and then a film again in the evening.

I did not text Michael that day or any time over Christmas. It was the first Christmas we had never seen Michael at all. And, to be honest, much as he often angered and frustrated and infuriated me, I was sad about that. More than I would have imagined. It was not the best of Christmases, to be honest.

Thursday 27 December 2012

I went home on Christmas Eve and I spent some time in town for a while. Then it was Christmas Day and I wasn't up for it at all. I spent it with Niamh's family, but really I wanted to be with my own family. I'm hoping that Christmas will be better in the future. Christmas Day was okay but it didn't feel like Christmas to me. I really just wanted it to be over. I just want to be on my own at the moment. I need some space. I wish I'd seen my family – it might have felt more Christmassy but I don't like my family seeing me not well.

* * *

Today I feel pretty bad because I had to pack my stuff up to come back to the Priory. I have had a meeting with Dr Webster which went well, though.

My weight is now 50.8 kilos. I also just got told that I'm going to get leave again! That was a nice boost. I get to go home again tomorrow morning, which is awesome. I feel like I'm making some sort of progress.

Wilko isn't feeling good at all. His leave didn't go well and I can see he's struggling. I have spent a lot of time talking to him and he told me a little more about his horrible past and some really bad things that happened to him which I think have scarred him pretty badly.

* * *

I get to have five nights' leave! This is a massive step forward for me, considering I have gone for huge stretches of time just sitting alone in my room here. I come back on Wednesday for my CPA (care plan assessment) on Thursday. Niamh will be picking me up tomorrow. I just want to spend as much time as I can away from here.

I have been talking to Petra this evening about the possibility of getting discharged. I'm hopeful, but I know I could get knocked down if I don't get what I want. I also really want to see my family now because I haven't seen them properly in ages. My weight is going up pretty fast and isn't slowing down, which feels weird and scary and I don't feel in control about that.

Friday 28 December 2012

Today I'm getting picked up and I get to go home for five nights, which is brilliant! I have to have breakfast first before I go, though.

I'm hoping we have a good New Year – and surely next year can't be as awful as this year. I don't think anything could ever be as bad as this year.

This past year has just been one massive nightmare, to be honest. I can't even really remember parts of it – my mind is just blank. Maybe it's been so dreadful that my brain blots out the worst of it to protect me. I don't know – I hope that's the case; otherwise, I am probably experiencing dementia. I almost died in hospital, I couldn't walk and I ended up in the loony bin.

Sunday 30 December 2012

I am on leave now but am still keeping a diary. I think it's a good thing to do, so maybe one day I will look back on it. It's really nice to be out and at home. I came home on Friday and had dinner. We had a veggie pasta bake. I have been catching up on *Game of Thrones*, so I have been binge-watching that. I always think I will sit down to watch one episode, but before I know it I've started the sixth. It's beginning to feel a bit more normal being back at home and I like having a little more control of my life. I could shake things up and do something mental. Or maybe not.

Tuesday 1 January 2013

A new diary – a proper one this time, not a notebook.

Yesterday I laid in and then I had lunch at home. I had couscous with tofu and I then did some gaming and generally chilled out. It's hard knowing that I have to pack my stuff away soon to head back to rehab. I'm still bingeing on *Game of Thrones*. Going back to rehab will pull me back down and it makes me realise how much I want to be out now.

Hopefully, my meeting on Thursday will go well and I will get some positive feedback. I hope to hear some kind of news on when I will be leaving. Also, it's getting hard to keep writing this diary in the Priory when all I do there is eat, sleep and cry and eat, sleep and cry and...eat, sleep and cry. I feel like there needs to be an exciting plot twist. Maybe a murder?

I hope I'm not still writing this diary by the time I get to the last page. Or at least I hope I am still not here.

Wednesday 2 January 2013

I'm now back at the Priory. I feel so lonely here, even though there are lots of people milling about. I have a weigh-in tomorrow, which I'm feeling extremely nervous about because I want it to be positive for my meeting with Dr Webster.

* * *

It feels like it's been a while since I've seen the other crazies in here and it's starting to feel odd. There's a sense of jealously in the air towards me. I have felt it myself in the past towards people who have had the chance to go home for a while when I haven't. I'm just about to go to dinner, so I will see how the others are there.

* * *

The others were okay with me. They were a lot quieter than usual, but it's probably just because I've been away and not so much a part of the group.

Thursday 3 January 2013

Today is my sister's birthday and it really sucks that I have to be locked up in here.

I had my weigh-in this morning which went well. When I say it went well, I mean I stuffed myself enough to please the doctors. I went up from 48.0 kilos to 49.5. I think that will please Dr Webster. I have my CPA meeting today which I'm getting very nervous about because they don't come around very often and can determine what happens in the coming months.

I feel like I have a migraine coming on, which isn't good. It's probably because I've been stressing myself about things. I'm not good at much but I am good at stressing. If there were an Olympic sport for it, I would have a whole trophy cabinet full of gold medals. In fact, I'd probably have won bronze, silver and gold at the same time.

* * *

I've just had lunch with the other inmates before heading back to my room. I saw Colm earlier – he is the guy who oversees me and will check up on me when I eventually get out of here. He's fine, but he has never had any mental health issues himself as far as I know, so I don't really take much notice of what he says. For me, people who have experienced mental health issues understand. Those who haven't, don't. It's as simple as that. I'm not being nasty; it's just how it is. He's a lovely guy, but I might as well be talking to some random stranger at the pub.

Niamh and her mum will be here soon for my big meeting. They will just sit in and listen to what has to be said. The meeting is basically a more serious assessment of how I am doing. I know for a fact that people only get discharged at these meetings and they don't happen very often. I'm starting to get nervous because I don't know what's going to happen. I want to get discharged now – TODAY – but I know I will feel crushed if I don't.

STRESS EXERCISE 1: THE SHRINKING WIDESCREEN TV

We're trying to present this first part of the book in as straightforward a manner as we can, mainly by following Michael's diary pretty much day by day so that you can see a little of what goes on inside the head of someone with mental illness.

We're then – for parents, family and loved ones – trying to offer the Maitland family's views at key points in Michael's story. If you have a loved one somewhere along the path to mental illness, it may help you to know you're not alone. Maybe we can also offer you some ideas that may shorten the journey or perhaps take it along another, nicer path.

We're also trying to drop in some how-to suggestions for exercises that can be done for those experiencing mental health issues – basic at this stage, more detailed later on – so that there are practical benefits for you. We tend to include these as and when Michael raises relevant points in his diary, so we may jump about a little depending on what's happening to him and his mood at the time.

Stress, as such, is something we've not written about, but clearly this is now an issue for Michael (and in reality has been for some time). So we will offer some suggestions over the next few pages. The first, long-used exercise, which works for many, can be called 'the TV trick'.

Start by imagining you have a big, widescreen TV in front of you, with a top-of-the-range, cutting-edge picture. Whatever it is that is causing stress can be seen on that TV in big, bold colours.

What you then need to do is to imagine you are draining all the colour out of that picture until it is black and white. Now shrink that picture, smaller and smaller, until you can barely see it at all. Hold it there, so small and insignificant.

You are controlling your stress. That's good. If you can, now see if you can slowly make that picture bigger again, going through black and white and into colour, with a more positive, upbeat picture that makes you feel good. This is such a simple trick and it works well as a quick fix for many sufferers.

Friday 4 January 2013

I DIDN'T GET OUT. I FEEL CRUSHED, COMPLETELY CRUSHED.

Saturday 5 January 2013

I didn't get discharged and I didn't write this stupid diary either. Not until now, anyway. I've calmed down. Just a little bit. I still feel stressed out.

The meeting did not go well. I cried at one point, which always makes me look mentally unstable. I then went on to lose my temper with various staff members, which made me seem angry and aggressive and that's never much help either.

I cried and lost my temper because I'm fed up of this place, these people, my life. I can't describe how frustrating it is being stuck here, how lonely it is. I've been lonely for too long.

* * *

I feel bad now for what I said, but I'm feeling incredibly frustrated and very angry with everyone. I'm extremely low and want to just give up on everything.

I got to go home for the weekend, but when I go back, I know I will be locked up for much longer than I expected. It's starting to break me down being at the Priory and I really feel like I'm never going to get out permanently. The meeting kind of ruined the trip home as I know I'll have to spend even longer wading through this endless crap.

STRESS EXERCISE 2: THROWING THE SWITCH

This exercise – we've heard it called 'throwing the switch' by some – is a variation on the TV exercise we mentioned a page or two ago. It's another visualisation exercise that's easy to do. As with all these exercises, you have to 'get into' them – when you do, you'll find they work much better.

Shut your eyes and imagine you are standing outside a house at night. It's a nice house, one you like. You can design it yourself in your head. Maybe make it a standard, four-bed detached house or a sweet country cottage. Somewhere you'd like to live.

You are standing outside and it is dark – or at least dim – and you are looking up at the windows. It's dark inside too. But it is a nice dark – a dim twilight rather than pitch black. You move to the front door and push it open and move inside.

You then move towards the top of the basement stairs. You look down and at the bottom of the stairs, across the basement floor, are all your problems and worries. You can stand there and see them in that dim twilight.

You now walk down the stairs and, as you get towards the bottom, you reach out and turn on the light switch. The basement, the stairs and everything above you are filled with a warm, golden light.

Look again at your problems and worries and see how small and insignificant they are. You could pretty much brush them away into the corners of that basement. You could do just that now with the broom that's leaning against the wall.

You now walk back up the stairs and each room is bathed in this warm light. All is good. All is well. Those problems and worries are not troubling you any more; they are now swept away and forgotten about. When you are ready, open your eyes, feeling better about yourself.

Sunday 6 January 2013

Today started just as it always does. I woke up, had breakfast, washed in the shower, looked with self-hatred in the mirror, put on my clothes and popped into town.

I met up with my mum, dad and brother at the last minute for a drink in Costa. They got me a couple of things, a DVD and a book, which was really nice of them and I loved getting to see them – always a nice boost.

I'm now back at the Priory, alone in my room, back to this dreary reality. It's getting harder coming back here each time. I hate it. I don't think I'll ever find doing this easy, no matter how long I'm here for. Ward round isn't for a few days yet, so I need to somehow get myself back into the day-to-day routine of boredom.

Stress exercise 3: A bird in flight

If there is a particular problem that is stressing you, an exercise that can be effective is what we might call 'a bird in flight.' It has echoes of the last two exercises.

Sit somewhere comfortable where you can shut your eyes and breathe in slowly and regularly for a few minutes. Your problem, whatever it is, is in a little box by the side of the road outside your house. Now, in your mind's eye, imagine you are a bird and you are taking off, swooping and soaring into the sky. Higher and higher you fly.

Look down at your house, your road and that now-tiny box below you. See how small everything appears as you fly up and up. The people, all stressed and hurrying about, are like ants, perhaps even smaller than that – dots.

Fly even higher. All you can now see below you is the warm blue sky and soft white clouds. You cannot see the world below or anything there that was troubling you.

Your problem, whatever it was, is the tiniest of specks and you can imagine, up here in the clouds, that it has been blown away on the wind, far, far away, and will never been seen again. It's gone. You're free. When you are ready, breathe out and open your eyes.

Monday 7 January 2013

Waking up here in the Priory is like waking up into a nightmare instead of waking from one. I dream about nice things before realising where I am. I've just been weighed: 50.3 kilos. It's a good thing that it's going up because it means I'm closer to getting out.

I have no idea what is happening for the rest of the day. I think I might be seeing the body coach woman. I'm feeling low again and really just trying to make it all the way through to bedtime so I can shut down again. I'm getting bad headaches because I have lots of normal coffee at home, but when I get back here I have to have decaf which gives me withdrawal symptoms.

I'm also starting to feel pretty heavy in myself. That, combined with feeling homesick, isn't making me feel great overall. I'm finding it hard to motivate myself to do anything. I just want to sleep and not talk to anyone. When I get back from leave, I find it really hard to fit back in with the others, which means I feel even more alone.

I felt so down this afternoon so I just slept. I then went and had a bath and slept some more. I'm in my room now, waiting for Niamh to turn up. I want to find out when my next leave will be.

* * *

Niamh came for dinner. We both had brie and beetroot tart. We chilled out and watched *Big Brother* in my room. I talked to Niamh at dinner about stuff. We go through phases of feeling like we are stronger, but, at other times, I feel like this is breaking us. When she left, I did a few drawings of myself to sum up how I feel.

I'VE ALWAYS DRAWN MYSELF A LOT AS A WAY OF EXPRESSING FEELINGS DEEP DOWN INSIDE.

Tuesday 8 January 2013

This morning I woke up feeling very sad. It's just knowing I'm still doing all of this for a lot longer. I still cry a lot but I now try to do it when no one is about. It's very much a game here and any signs of weakness are recorded and held against you, however much the staff try to say they won't. I know that now and I know how to play the game. I try to act 'normal' – i.e. 'happy' or at least 'happy-ish' –

in front of them and keep my crying and stuff out of sight.

* * *

I think I have CBT this morning and yoga this afternoon. I know it's better for me to stay busy, but some days can be a real struggle to get motivated to do anything.

* * *

I decided not go to yoga. I just rested in my room. I'm anxious. I need something positive to happen because it's all getting a bit much at the moment.

STRESS EXERCISE 4: THE LIGHT AT THE END OF THE TUNNEL

There is an exercise – we've heard it called 'the light at the end of the tunnel' – that can be beneficial for many people.

Close your eyes and imagine you are in total darkness. You cannot see anything – ahead, behind, above, below – although you can feel yourself standing on hard, gravelly ground.

Look ahead and, after a minute or two of regular, steady breathing, imagine you can see a pinprick of light a little way away in the distance.

You decide to walk slowly towards it. As you do, you see that pinprick get ever so slightly larger. And larger again as you get closer. And larger still.

You can then, ever so slowly, start to make out that you are in a tunnel. That light is bright enough to reveal the ceiling and the walls and the floor of the tunnel.

Eventually, as you continue walking steadily towards it, sunlight starts to flood in, until you can even see the brickwork and moss of the tunnel ceiling and walls, and the stones beneath your feet.

You can see beyond the end of the tunnel, towards the warmth and the sunlight and a field of gently moving wheat. You move out into it. You can feel the sunlight on your eyelids, the sun on your arms, the breeze on your face. As you come back into the real world, as and when you are ready, bring this sense of peace with you.

Wednesday 9 January 2013

I saw the doctor yesterday, which went okay. He said that my next leave will probably be Thursday to Sunday of this week. I wanted to ask him if I could have Sunday night at home as well. I didn't get a chance to ask because I forgot in the last meeting and we rarely get to see him. Even if he does pop by, he likes to avoid talking to us.

* * *

I'm now allowed 'free fluids'. Writing that down seems so weird, but it means that I can get drinks any time I like. It doesn't sound like much, but when you have been so limited for so long it's a nice treat.

I'm also allowed to have snacks in my room. When I say we are limited, I mean we are allowed one hot drink with a meal, one cold drink with each meal or snack and that's pretty much it. For snacks, I can now choose what I like, but they have to be okayed. I had a packet of crisps and sat and watched *Peep Show*.

* * *

I think we have a trip out today (rehab). I think that we will be having lunch in the lodge. Niamh is also allowed to come for dinner tonight.

STRESS EXERCISE 5: THE WORRY STONE

This exercise is effective for some, Michael included. Once he left the Priory, he told me he kept a little red food token from there in his pocket at all times. I wondered why and asked him. It was his 'worry stone'; that is the word used to describe it by many mental health experts. Here's how it works.

Close your eyes, breathe deeply and try to create a sense of calm in and around you. Imagine you have a stone, a pebble or maybe a crystal in the palm of your hand. This can be a real one or you can imagine one in your favourite colour and texture – warm, blue, shiny, perhaps. It's up to you.

Now focus on what is troubling you and have that thought held in the middle of your forehead. Now, when you are ready and feel able to do it, you have to mentally push that worry down and along your arm, through into your hand and fingers until it is pushed into the stone, until it is all soaked up.

You could even imagine washing the stone – it works for some and maybe for you. You literally rub at whatever it is – a stone, a little red food token – with your thumb over and over again, washing that worry away. Try it – this is something that many people do and it works well for them.

Thursday 10 January 2013

Not a good day. My weight had dropped. This means I might not be able to go home on leave. I now have to wait to meet Dr Webster at ward round later; not looking forward to that.

* * *

I went to a different group for depression today which was outside of my unit. It mainly involved talking to others and getting an insight into their issues. The staff here encourage talking about stuff as much as possible. I hate it, though. I don't like people. I don't like talking. It took place in another building and had a mix of all different types of inpatients based here.

It was pretty unsettling – there were some very different types of people, from drug users to sex addicts. Even with all that going on, my mind was elsewhere. There was one guy that came in who's in the City and only comes in on this day. He's a drug addict and looked totally out of it to me. He talked about some pretty horrific stuff he's done and made me realise some people live such different lives to me.

* * *

I have just seen the doctor. I still get to go home but I get two nights instead of three. It's a blow but at least I still get out for a bit. It seems unfair because I haven't done anything wrong; it's just that my weight hasn't gone up the way it should have done. Again, this is where it all feels like a game. It's all numbers. Up and I get longer out. Down and I get less time out. No matter what's going on in my head.

STRESS EXERCISE 6: THE WARM SANDY BEACH

Some experts suggest a way to handle general stress and ill-at-ease-ness (if there is such a word) is to set aside ten minutes, whenever you feel down, to sit or lie somewhere quiet, shut your eyes and just daydream about whatever makes you feel calm and relaxed.

A favourite is where you are on a golden, sandy beach, somewhere warm with a gentle breeze and palm trees swaying and the blue sea lapping softly at your feet. It's quiet and peaceful, and you are just going to lie here and let everything drift away from you.

You may want to try other 'at peace' moments that are personal to you. You may imagine yourself by a stream or a river, in a meadow, in your back garden, on a hillside – anywhere that is warm and peaceful, and where you can shut your eyes and let everything float off into the sky.

Sunday 13 January 2013

I sometimes 'forget' to write in my diary when I'm at home because I'm trying to make the most of the time I have, whereas when I am back here (in the Priory) I have so much time sitting alone in my room that I might as well keep writing.

Yesterday, Niamh and I went into town and had to do a few shopping bits. It's nice to do normal things again, even if it feels like make-believe. We then went home and watched TV and had a veggie pasta bake.

I always hate having to come back to the Priory after being allowed out. I hope that this next week doesn't feel as slow as last week and my weigh-ins go okay.

Monday 14 January 2013

I was weighed this morning – 50.6 kilos. I have gone up, which is good and at least it will please Dr Webster.

It gets me so down waking up here. The feeling is so horrible. I don't like the atmosphere and it's hard to not let it get to you. There's a new girl here called Susi. I haven't had a chance to really talk to her yet, but she seems nice.

* * *

I think Niamh might be coming for dinner today.

* * *

I have been sitting in my room watching YouTube videos over and over again. It's a complete waste of time but it makes me laugh, so I don't care.

I had better go and join the queue with the other lunatics for meds. I'm hoping the day passes quickly today – I could ask them to double my dosage and just feel dazed for the rest of the day.

RELAXATION EXERCISE 1: THE LIGHTED CANDLE

The self-help exercises we've been suggesting for anger, anxiety and worry and stress and, in a moment, relaxation are all easy to do. Clearly, though, they are low-level and you are not going to turn around clinical depression – as Michael had when he was in the Priory – by shouting 'Stop!' at the top of your voice or by rubbing a stone. Even so, they work for some. Let's look, over the next few pages, at some low-level relaxation ideas that work for many people. We have tried the ones we mention and they are effective for us.

One that works for many involves sitting somewhere quiet and peaceful, with a lighted candle in front of you. You need to focus on the candle and try to breathe slowly and regularly, shutting out as many of your thoughts as you can. Try to breathe as deeply as you can. Work yourself into a relaxing rhythm of breathing.

Close your eyes but hold the image of that gentle and peaceful flame in the front of your mind. Keep breathing deeply and steadily. When you are ready, imagine the flame entering your mind and, as you breathe slowly in and out, moving into your body. It feels warm and relaxing. You might, with practice, begin to feel that you and the flame are one and the same. You are absorbed into the flame. The flame is absorbed into you.

You should feel that the flame is part of you, and that, as you breathe in and out, it warms and relaxes different parts of your body in turn. Keep doing this for as long as you can, until your mind is empty and focused wholly on the flame.

When you feel ready, move your focus away from the flame and back on to your breathing, as if you are slowly withdrawing from the flame and separating from it. Once you have focused on your breathing, continue to breathe deeply for two or three minutes and then open your eyes.

Wednesday 16 January 2013

Yesterday was another hard day and I did not feel like writing my diary. I have been feeling pretty ill and I am not sure why. I have a bad toothache and it's making me feel run down. I just ate beans on toast.

I feel sad today. Again, I don't really know why. I think it's just realising how long I've been here and the frustration I feel being locked away. The weeks feel so long.

I'm nervous about the weigh-in tomorrow. It's not just me, though. Everyone is on edge when weigh-in is coming up because it's probably the most crucial thing that the doctors and staff look at when they are assessing how well you are doing.

* * *

We went out for rehab to Starbucks and pretended to fit in with the normal folk. We then picked up bits for lunch to have at the lodge when we got back. I quite like walking into town now. I guess it is different and breaks the usual monotony. I have body image class this afternoon but I'm feeling really tired. Niamh can't make it in time for dinner tonight as she has to work late, but she will be here after.

Relaxation exercise 2:
One-two-three deep breaths

We've not really talked about the benefits of exercise in relation to such issues as anger, stress, anxiety and relaxation. But Michael mentions in his last entry, and he has alluded to it elsewhere, that he enjoyed walking. But not so much yoga, perhaps, although that may have had more to do with a sense of embarrassment. No matter; the key point here is that, for some people, mental health issues can be eased to some degree by physical activity, from Pilates or yoga through to long walks, running or swimming – whatever suits you.

> Yoga worked a little for Michael. A one-two-three deep breaths exercise learned at yoga can work well with long walks. You can take one, two, three steps as you breathe in, hold on to that breath for the next one, two, three steps (the number depending on your stride) and then release. A breathing/walking rhythm, with each breath and stride controlled by you, can be calming for many who try it.

Monday 21 January 2013

I haven't written for a few days because I have been away on leave and 'accidentally' left my diary behind. I got to go home on Friday. On the Sunday, I got to see my family and we went for a drink.

I had to come back to the Priory this morning instead of last night because there was heavy snow and we couldn't drive. We tried, but the roads were iced over and the car was slipping all over the place. We had to call the Priory and explain why I wasn't coming back. Hopefully, next time I'm out, it will snow as if it's Narnia and I'll never have to go back.

Tuesday 22 January 2013

The weigh-in this morning went well. I've gone from 49.8 to 50.5 kilos.

My meal plan has also increased. It basically just means more food is added to each meal and snack time. I'm on meal plan three.

With the meal plans, there is obviously breakfast, lunch and dinner with snacks in between. Meal plan increase involves adding a dessert to lunch at first and then one after dinner.

Then, as things increase, a snack is added after dinner as well. This also means that I can bring in my own snacks and stuff that I like to have. I can bring things from when I go out on leave, so I bring back crisps and cereal bars and stuff like that. You slowly get given more freedom – but not much.

Niamh is coming for dinner tonight, so I'm looking forward to that. It's weird; it feels as if, when she's coming for dinner, it's like a date, just in a mental institution, surrounded by lunatics.

I have my next CPA meeting booked for 7 February at 2.30pm. This will be where I sit down with Dr Webster and three nurses. They then look through my records and assess how mental I am and if I'm sane enough to be let loose. I hope to get out obviously, but I feel like I'm never leaving here now. I think if I were told I had to stay longer again, it might break me. I need to try to chill out.

RELAXATION EXERCISE 3: MEDITATING ON OM

Meditating on a sound or a word or a statement can be a good way to help you to relax. The sound or the word or the statement is your mantra, and repeating it again and again whilst you are in a relaxing state can be very beneficial.

Sit or lie, as you prefer, in a comfortable position somewhere quiet and peaceful. Close your eyes and focus your mind on your mantra. You choose this. It may be a word based on your personal beliefs such as 'Om'. Or you can choose a positive word such as 'love'. You may prefer to go with a two-syllable word or a phrase that allows you to get into a rhythm as you repeat it. It's your choice.

The mantra itself is not the key to this exercise but it is something that you can repeat over and again in time with your breathing. It is the mantra, repeated slowly again and again, that should still your mind from its endless thoughts. In many ways, the mantra becomes a droning noise that quietens your mind and tensions.

Wednesday 23 January 2013

Last night Niamh came for dinner, which was nice.

We are meant to have our trip out today, but the snow is pretty bad and I don't think they will let us loose.

I have been here for a long time now.

* * *

We did get to go out! That was nice. We went to Costa for a drink and, as usual, the staff watched us closely. It's weird as new patients join the Priory and come out. It makes me realise how much I've changed since I first got here. Also, I can see how the staff have to keep such a close eye on them. I can see how much I've changed by looking at the new patients who come in. They are really bad and I know I must have been like that, if not worse.

Maybe I'm getting better.

The new guys looked scared and they probably should be because what they are about to experience is horrible and will make them feel worse in some ways. If they hate their looks/bodies now, then there's a lot more to come. I have gained some confidence since I've been here and I will actually talk to people now. At first I didn't want to talk to anyone. I would just hide away in my room and cry, to be honest. I do actually talk to staff now.

* * *

For the rest of the day I'm going to try to relax a bit. I have been feeling edgy, so I want to just sit in my room and put on a film. I love watching films and always have. I like watching films like *Alice in Wonderland*, *Star Wars* and comedies to take my mind off the fact I want to kill myself (only joking).

I'm trying to practise doing a bit of meditation to help clear my mind. I think meditation is a good way to relax in general but especially for people who have busy minds. It certainly helps. It's a simple way of calming the mind and body.

Relaxation exercise 4: 7/11 breathing

Michael used a breathing technique known as 7/11. The 7/11 technique is a breathing exercise where you breathe in for a count of 7 and out for a count of 11.

Again, as with the candle exercise and the mantra meditation, you need to find somewhere that you can feel calm and peaceful and can switch off for a few minutes. We've talked of breathing exercises and these have tended to be very balanced: breathing in and out, perhaps through different nostrils, a set number of times each. This 7/11 is slightly different in that you breathe in and count to seven and then breathe out for the count of 11.

Michael used it help him relax and gain or regain his composure in a variety of situations. It helped him to calm down and relax if he was feeling stressed or even when he was lonely. It's just about getting into a peaceful state of mind. Even the simplest of exercises can work – even with someone as troubled as Michael.

Thursday 24 January 2013

I was weighed this morning and that went well. I'm now at 50.7 kilos. I think I will be getting my leave tomorrow morning until Monday evening, which will be nice. I have also seen how other patients get unsupervised meals, so I hope I get those soon. That's basically where you get to sit and eat alone or with the other patients with the same privileges.

* * *

Today, I have the depression group again. This is where a real mix of people meet up from different units and even some outpatients. These can be addicts, whether it's sex, alcohol or drugs.

There was an outpatient that came in who to me looked like he was off his face. He was raging about his ex and saying he's got millions and could easily fly away and leave this place. He works in the City and is addicted to cocaine. He also clearly has some severe anger issues. It is always a bit scary being near him. I sat as far away from him as possible. I'm feeling okay at the moment for a change.

RELAXATION EXERCISE 5: ONE PART AT A TIME

If you can relax, with whatever works for you, it will go some way to handling all sorts of related mental health issues – stress and anger, for example. When Michael did yoga, he did an exercise like this.

Sit down or lie – whatever suits you – on the ground. You should have your legs stretched out in front of you. Breathe slowly in and out, and focus on this breathing for two minutes. Breathing well is a key part of relaxing and eliminating many negative thoughts.

You then need to focus on relaxing each part of your body in turn. You can start with your feet. Then imagine your legs relaxing, and your lower body. Work your way steadily up through to your chest and arms, shoulders and neck, and eventually your head and face.

Some people find it helps to chant or just gently repeat to themselves a phrase such as 'I am relaxing'. Others prefer to imagine their body feeling light and airy, as if all their troubles are lifting up and floating away.

You can end this exercise by returning your focus to your breathing. Breathe slowly in and out again and concentrate on this for two minutes.

As you will see as we progress through the book, we are great believers in people finding their own solutions rather than following a one-size-fits-all remedy. That's not to say that your own solution should be at the cost of proper medical and professional advice, just that you can vary these self-help exercises to suit yourself. Some may feel right for you, others not. And you may want to jig them so they feel a better fit for you. With this one, for example, you don't have to breathe for exactly two minutes – do what feels right for you.

Friday 25 January 2013

This morning my dad is picking me up. Before that, I have unsupervised breakfast, which will be weird, but nice to chill out. I'm also excited to go home on leave.

I also have to get my meds and run through the risk assessment before I can go today.

I'm excited to get home and chill out. I think I will ask my dad to stop at Tesco on the way back so I can pick up a few bits and pieces.

Tuesday 29 January 2013

I went home on Friday and walked into town to get some bits and pieces. In the evening, I had a veggie lasagne with Niamh. On Saturday, I went and saw my parents in town. Me, Adam and Niamh went round the shops and Adam got a Wii U. In the evening, we went home and had a veggie quiche, which was nice, and we chilled out and watched some TV. I'm really into *Dexter*. I think I like watching it because the main character is weird and different from other people. I like watching things where there are people who differ from the norm.

Monday, I was on my own because Niamh had work. I just chilled out at home and made sure I relaxed before knowing I had to get ready to come back. Being at home is nice, but it also makes me miss it so much more when I have to come back here. I think them sending me home is not only testing me to see how I do but also to make me realise what I'm missing.

I was weighed this morning and I came in at 53.4 kilos. I'm really feeling uncomfortable in my skin at the moment and the fact our weight is drilled into our heads the whole time doesn't help.

I have CBT and a one-to-one with Richard later. I had breakfast on my own, which is good but also a bit lonely sitting alone whilst the others are together. Having breakfast on my own does show that I'm making progress at least.

There are a couple of new people here now. There's a lady called Jenna who looks really ill. She's one of the thinnest people I've ever seen and, because of that, she struggles to walk. I think this is the fourth time she's been here now – I'm never coming back here, I'll make sure of that.

There's also a younger girl called Terri. I think she's also been here before. I can't imagine getting out and then having to come back one day. I don't think I could take that.

PICKING MICHAEL UP AND TALKING

For a long time now, I had felt as though I – the whole family really – was not part of Michael's life any more. There was contact – letters and parcels, emails and stuff – but we did not see him that much. Tracey and I had visited him in the Priory in mid-December, but we had not seen him at all over Christmas and had only really met him once or twice since then to have coffee in Ipswich with Niamh.

It all felt rather distant, especially never getting to see Michael on his own. I am sure many parents will feel that, however well you get on with your children's partners (and we have a mixed track record, to be honest), it is nice now and then to have them to yourselves – just the original family members. (That's probably best kept as a thought rather than saying it out loud, though.)

So, when I knew Michael was coming out regularly, and that Niamh and her mother were both at work on Friday morning, and I was only sitting at home staring out to sea thinking of something or other to write, I offered to run down and pick him up and take him home to Ipswich. I thought it would give us a chance to talk (and I could also stop off and have a Big Breakfast at the McDonalds down the road from the Priory before I arrived there at 10am).

I'm not one for offering advice as such – if you've read this far, you'll know I'd not win 'Dad of the Year'. But if I did offer advice to anyone with a loved one who has mental health issues, it's this: talking and listening (with the emphasis on you listening and them talking) is so important and plays a key role in that person getting better, relationships being rebuilt and things just working out as you'd want them to do.

And so, rather nicely, it proved for us. I picked Michael up, without giving too much of the story away in advance, for one or two Friday mornings. All I ever did was to run him home, via a supermarket so he could get a bit of shopping (like royalty, Michael never carries cash) or via another route (when the A12 was blocked). We only spent 30 or 40 minutes together each time, but we did talk things through. It was a bit awkward at first. I remember saying, 'I always thought it was Niamh,' whilst looking away from him, and Michael replying, 'No, she always wanted to be friends with everyone.'

The great advantage of talking in a car is that you sit side by side, so you don't need to make eye contact but can still have a conversation. From there, our conversation ranged over various subjects – in essence, why, when and how it all happened – and I felt that I had a better understanding of Michael and him of me. If there is such a thing as a 'balloon of anger' – filled with mutual misunderstanding, confusion, disappointment and frustration – the air was slowly let out of it over these weeks. I felt that things were much better between us over that time and that was a big plus moving forward.

Wednesday 30 January 2013

Last night, Niamh came for dinner. We had stuffed peppers and chips. Dr Webster has decided to change my leave from now on. He wants to give me two nights at the weekend and one during the week. I'm not really sure what to think about that and whether it's good or bad. I think it's meant to be good. At least it will break the week up a bit. I can also now have unsupervised lunches, which is good. My CPA meeting is next week.

* * *

I just had breakfast. I'm now back in my room. I'm feeling lonely at the moment, to be honest. I'm thinking about my weigh-in tomorrow and really hope it goes okay because I want to go on leave at the weekend. I will just try to stay busy today as much as I can. That can be difficult in here, though.

* * *

I keep myself busy by drawing lots, watching films and having chats with the other patients. I was talking to Petra who has been here for years. God's sake, I'd better not be here that bloody long. I reckon she must be pretty brain-dead from being here so long. I know I'd go even more insane.

RELAXATION EXERCISE 6: THE ETERNAL FLAME

We have spoken already about the role of a candle exercise in terms of relaxation and we have talked about breathing exercises as well. The eternal flame exercise is one we have come across over the years that combines the two and can be effective. You may find it a good way to start and end the day, and possibly at points in between when you want to relax.

Again, sit or lie down in a comfortable position. Sitting seems more sensible for this exercise as a candle is involved, but many people do it lying on their back, using their imagination more. It is a pretend candle, after all. Imagine there is a candle flame about six inches (15 centimetres) from your lips. What you are going to do is to breathe out and in without blowing the candle out.

Breathe out slowly and gently as if you are emptying your lungs of all of your air, but so carefully that you do not blow out the flame. Count to see how many seconds it takes you to expel your breath.

You now need to breathe back in – again, slowly and steadily, so that you do not suck out that flame, and keep going until your lungs are full. Count to yourself as you are doing this to see how long this lasts.

Keep doing this, for something like 30 times each. As you increase the number – and you may want to start slowly and build up – you should start to feel yourself relaxing. As always, do what feels best for you. There is no 'right' and 'wrong'; play around with the exercise to suit you.

Friday 1 February 2013

Today is the first of February and I can't really believe how long I've been here: one way or the other since November.

Yesterday wasn't a good day as my head wasn't in the right place, so I did not write anything.

My weight had dropped to 52.9 kilos.

I've felt very anxious and upset all day. The doctor took away all unsupervised privileges apart from my evening snack. I'm feeling pretty low at the moment.

Monday 4 February 2013

I went home for the weekend. My dad came and got me on Friday morning and took me back to my house in Ipswich. I relaxed at home and waited for Niamh to get in from work. For dinner, Niamh made a pasta bake. It's so nice to be able to sleep in my own bed.

On Saturday morning, we went to the cinema to see *Flight*, which I really enjoyed. Then we went into town as usual and got a coffee. I like just doing simple things when I'm back at home; it makes me more relaxed.

On Sunday, we went and got a new TV! That was cool and I don't normally go and buy things like that; even small things for myself is a challenge. We needed it, though, as our other TV was broken. I love Niamh and I feel so bad for putting us through all this endless crap.

I'm back at the Priory (obviously, I don't write my diary at home now). I'm nervous about seeing Dr Webster again. I'm hoping that, after losing weight last time round, I get my unsupervised privileges back.

There's a new staff member - God, she's so annoying. I also think she doesn't have a clue how to treat anorexics. We were at dinner and sometimes the staff eat with us. One staff member turned to her and said, 'Do you want a dessert?' and she said, 'No, I'd better not because I don't want to get fat.' I burst out laughing.

Some staff are better than others. There is one member of staff called Sam who is always very kind to me. Being shut away in your room for hours on end is horrible. Sam always pops in my room and takes the time to talk to me. Nothing in particular, but she just makes an effort to make sure I am≈okay.

There was a guy called David who left halfway through my time here. I had a lot of chats with him. I think he liked having a guy to chat to who probably wasn't too far off his age. He said he had been working there a while and it's uncommon to have two male inpatients at the same time.

The staff in general are fairly good and know what they are doing. The night staff, on the other hand, are terrible. They sit about during the night, playing music, smoking and chatting loudly. Some of them don't speak English. I remember Liv having a full-blown argument with one of them in the middle of the night, so I came out of my room, sat on the sofa and watched it unfold. Neither of them were happy. I quite enjoyed it, though.

RELAXATION EXERCISE 7: TAKING
MOMENTS THROUGH THE DAY

As Michael comes towards the end of his stay in the Priory, we can see – for most of the time, anyway – a marked improvement in what he writes and how he phrases it. Much of the anger and anxiety and stress of the early days is, if not gone, at least not as overwhelming for him, and there are signs that he could relax a little and maybe even make a joke or two.

We have suggested a number of relaxation exercises. Let's end what we have to say about relaxation with some general suggestions.

Try to have times and places when and where you can relax at different points of the day; if you monitor your moods over a while, you may find that you'll get to know when you are most likely to need to take time out. Plan ahead if you can.

Ideally, you may want to take out ten minutes at a time to relax: before work, at lunchtime, after a commute home, perhaps. At home, you may find it easy to create a place to relax – a bedroom, quiet and peaceful and free from distractions. At work, you may have to find a quiet corner or a park bench.

Try an exercise that suits you. Shutting your eyes often helps if you can find something to focus on in your mind's eye, such as a flame.

As the day comes to an end, it can be a good idea to try to wind down slowly. Avoiding food and drink, especially coffee and alcohol, and any brain-stimulating activities such as gaming, using your mobile or even the television can be helpful.

Find ways that help you relax. We can suggest a short list. No doubt you can too. A bath, meditation, candles, soft music, reading a book, some gentle exercises – all can be effective and help you to unwind. The secret is to discover what works for you.

Tuesday 5 February 2013

Yesterday I found out that I get leave tonight and come back tomorrow after dinner. I also get another snack and meal unsupervised again.

* * *

I had breakfast this morning with Lesley, which was nice. She's short and looks scary, but once you talk to her you realise she's very caring. Lesley is the nicest person I've met here. She has had such a difficult life going in and out of rehab. She told me about being in rehab when she was very young and being force-fed.

I didn't want to ask her too much about her past because I know she's been through a lot as it is. She still has issues leaving her home and in some ways I think she finds comfort in being here.

Thursday 7 February 2013

I went home on Tuesday evening, which was nice. I got to spend Wednesday at home and I really enjoyed being able to relax. Niamh came home from work and we had some dinner.

It was then time to go back to the Priory and that was as awful a moment as ever.

I was weighed this morning and I'm now at 54.2 kilos. I have my CPA meeting today which I'm nervous about. I'm hoping to get an idea of a discharge date. I have unsupervised breakfast this morning before heading over to my depression group. I think it's my fifth week of doing it regularly.

Friday 8 February 2013

I had my CPA meeting yesterday. They have decided to change my leave again. I'm now going to go home on Fridays after tea and come back after tea on Sunday. I will also go home on Monday after tea until Wednesday after tea. So I'm getting a lot of time at home now. Niamh is coming for dinner tonight and then I get to go home. I'm about to go and have breakfast with Lesley, which I enjoy.

Monday 11 February 2013

I went home on Friday after dinner.

On Saturday, we went to the cinema to see *I Give It a Year*, which was really funny. We didn't do much else apart from chill out. On Sunday I saw my mum and dad for a bit, which was nice.

I got back to the Priory and have been weighed. I'm now at 55.3 kilos. Hopefully, my next ward round will go okay.

Thursday 14 February 2013

Weigh-in. From 55.3 to 55.9 kilos!

I went home for two nights and came back last night. I'm really back and forth at the moment, so writing my diary is all over the place. It was really nice to be home again.

I have another ward round today and as usual I want to find out about my next leave.

Today is Valentine's Day. At least I got to spend some time with Niamh. I hid chocolates all around the house for her, got her flowers and made her a card.

POSITIVITY EXERCISE 3:
SEE YOURSELF CONFIDENT

As we come towards the end of Part One of the book, I want to introduce one or two 'coming soon' themes – just to give you a heads-up on the sort of issues that Michael would face as he, at some stage soon, would leave the Priory and go back out into the world to do his master's, maybe get a part-time job and then a full-time job, and, eventually, to live a full and happy life.

One theme will be self-confidence – it is one thing to conquer your mental health demons to the point of what we might call equilibrium, but to then keep going and suddenly become self-confident is not easy. One exercise to do with confidence works on the basis that even if you don't feel very confident, you should try to act confident and, maybe one day, you will then feel confident. My advice to Michael has always been, in my own heavy-handed way, along the same lines: 'Imagine what a normal person would do – and do that; that'll fool them.' Funnily enough, and more by luck than judgement, it's not too far from being good advice.

So here's the exercise. You can start by listing the things that worry you; in this context, we are talking about getting back out into the real world, mixing with people, working, socialising, etc. All the 'normal' things in life that are anything but normal for those with mental health issues. Once you have your list, you can work through each point in turn.

There are many things that make people anxious and worried – and we could probably list pages and pages of our own here (as could you) – but we will suggest these general ones as examples: ordering a bottle of wine in a restaurant, meeting a partner's parents (or a child's partner) for the first time, going for an interview for that job you really want and giving a speech. Your own list may be endless.

Experts say much the same, although they dress it up in fancier terms. The how-to advice is that before

134

you do whatever it is, you imagine yourself doing it step by step and that it all goes really well. This gives you a framework to work to and may boost your confidence. So, you've been asked to say a few words about something you're working on; an essay, a report, maybe.

You prepare by looking over what you've been doing and pick out what you want to say and think through what you might be asked about. Before you speak, you work through the basic steps and what you are going to do, imagining it all in your head: what you might say and do at each moment. You then introduce yourself, and make eye contact and smile at whoever you're talking to. You are acting confident! You go over the main points, short and sweet, and sum it up. You ask if there are any questions, which you're prepared for, and answer them.

Friday 15 February 2013

I saw Dr Webster yesterday. I'm getting my normal weekend leave, and he said if that goes well, I will get an extended leave next week, which would be awesome. He also mentioned discharge which he has never done before!

I'm trying not to get my hopes up, though. I think it will feel so weird if and when I'm discharged.

I had breakfast with Lesley this morning. I like Lesley a lot and hope we manage to stay in contact. She lives with her dad who's very old and not very well.

Tuesday 19 February 2013

I had my usual leave at the weekend which went okay. Adam stayed over on Saturday, which was nice. We just hung out, played games and watched films.

I'm not feeling that good today. My weight is now 57.2. I'm starting to feel very ugly.

I saw Dr Webster yesterday which went okay, but I found out my next CPA isn't going to be until 7 March. I'm finding it quite difficult at the moment, but I just need to hold on and keep going. I get leave tomorrow until Sunday, so I get a bit longer which is good. I just can't believe how long I've been here.

Wednesday 20 February 2013

I'm going home today. My dad will be picking me up soon so I'm just waiting in my room.

I have been pretty down the last couple of days and I think it's making Niamh sad. I'm a bit worried to go home because I don't know if Niamh will even want me there.

Yesterday we had couples therapy. It was all pretty upsetting and I didn't like it. It just made me feel guilty. I feel like I've let her down. Sometimes I feel like she could do a lot better than me.

My dad will be here soon so I need to get my stuff ready. I need to try to relax.

POSITIVITY EXERCISE 4: SEE THE SILVER LINING

It's not simple for anyone, let alone someone with mental health problems, to stay positive all the time, and this – positivity – linked in with confidence, is another theme that we will cover in more detail in Part Two. One exercise that can help is called 'see the silver lining', or similar. It's a long-established, CBT-ish exercise that has a number of names and minor variations. In essence, it's a matter of looking at something that's worrying you in a structured and supportive way so that you can see the positives.

Take a sheet of paper and a pen or pencil and divide the sheet of paper into three equal columns. In the first column, write down whatever the matter is. For example, you might write 'Starting a job'. In the middle column, you list your concerns about this. Your list might include comments such as 'I feel anxious', 'Everyone will be looking at me', 'I don't know what to do', 'No one knows me.' It might be a long list, and that's fine.

In the third column – and this will take time to do if you have had or are suffering from mental ill-health – you list all the ways to rework the comments in the second column into more positive ones. You may want to do this reworking with a friend or family member who is cheerful and upbeat.

For example, 'No one knows me' sounds negative, but that can be reworked in several ways. Brainstorming lots of ideas, you might write 'I'm going to meet lots of new people who might become friends', 'Lots of people can help and support me and show me what to do' and so on. These are the positives you need to keep in mind. Positivity is so important – a key state of mind for getting better.

Monday 25 February 2013

I got to go home on Wednesday after rehab group and met Niamh at home. On Friday, I had to see Colm, who will work with me once I get out. He is a kind of mentor. Niamh came with me to see him and we had a chat about how I think I will do when I'm out. Niamh thinks I will probably get discharged soon, but I don't want to get my hopes up.

Me and my brother went to see *Wreck-It Ralph* at the cinema, which was actually really good. In the afternoon, Niamh and I went to see her dad, who I haven't seen in ages. We then came home and had dinner.

I was weighed this morning and I'm now 57.7 kilos. I hope I get to see Dr Webster early today. I really want to find out what's happening next. I've been here so long now.

I WANT MY LIFE BACK.

Tuesday 26 February 2013

I saw Dr Webster yesterday and I have had to step up my meal plan again. I have to stay here until

Thursday. If this week goes okay, then I get to go home for a week and then come back for the CPA meeting. I'm feeling very anxious, and when I go away on leave, it's very important that my weight goes up.

Wednesday 27 February 2013

Last night, Niamh came for dinner and we had vegetable kebabs and chips. Today is rehab day so we will be heading out into town. I'm being weighed tomorrow.

* * *

Rehab went well and I got to spend some time with Tippi. I've cracked my tooth and I'm in absolute agony, but there's nothing I can do. I have to just lie here in pain.

HAPPINESS EXERCISE: THE LIST OF TRUTHS

A third theme that we'll look at in Part Two of the book is that of 'being happy'. Michael, writing his dairy in the Priory, regularly lists things that make him happy, things that he misses very much such as sleeping in his own bed, chilling out, going for a walk. Hopefully, as and when he leaves the Priory, regaining these lost moments will bring him the happiness he craves.

Happiness, often, is not an easy thing to achieve. Many people think that they will become happy soon if they can just get that new job, move to a bigger place, earn some more money... It is always next month, next year and so on. It is always dependent on something happening that will improve their current lot, bring them more money or prestige. Michael, for all his woes in the Priory, did at least recognise that happiness often comes from the simplest of things.

It is only when something bad happens in their present situation – they lose their job, their partner leaves them, they have to move to a smaller place – that people suddenly realise they were happy all the time. The trick seems to be both to be happy and to know it.

Another CBT-ish exercise that is a good place to start is 'the list of truths'. Variations of this have been around for some time. This is simply a list of good things you have in your life which is written when you are feeling in an upbeat mood, perhaps alongside a family member or friend, and will help to balance out all the bad things that are probably in your mind when you need to read it.

It's up to you what's in the list but it might include the names of the people who love you, things that make you laugh, what you've done for other people lately, what other people have done for you, things that make you happy, something you are looking forward to. More to come in Part Two of the book. Happiness – it's what it's all about, when all's said and done.

Thursday 28 February 2013

My tooth is still killing me. I really need to see a
dentist.

* * *

The weigh-in went well – I'm now 58.4 kilos.
   I'm waiting to see Dr Webster. I'm not sure what
time I will see him today. I hope I see him soon.

* * *

I'M GOING HOME!

EMAILING DR WEBSTER

Behind the scenes, I did exchange a few emails with Dr Webster
through early 2013 just to check Michael was progressing
well. We ended our exchange like this…

Hi Mr Maitland

I am extremely pleased with Michael's progress and as I'm
sure you have noticed his true personality is returning and
his dependence on Niamh is abating.

   We are doing a lot of work around this and him eating
alone and he has been very humble and brave regarding
dealing with it.

   Thus, all in all, I feel he is doing very well; I am aiming
to discharge him and what's left of the disorder can be
dealt with in the community.

Dr Peter Webster

Hi

Thank you for everything you have done for Michael – although a simple thank you really doesn't do justice to how grateful we are.

Best wishes
Iain and Tracey Maitland

Hi Mr Maitland

It's been a real pleasure, particularly to see how his personality has grown and return to an adult. I am very pleased for you all and hope it all works out okay. If there's a slip-up we are always here. It must be lovely to have your son back!

All the best
Dr Peter Webster

So, there we were: Michael – a physically fit and mentally healthy Michael – was back after all these years.

ANOTHER FAIRY STORY

And so the Maitland family story came to a happy ending...

Michael left the Priory fit and well, and moved back to his home in Ipswich with his girlfriend, Niamh. He could look forward to resuming his master's degree in Moving Image and Sound at Norwich in the autumn. Work as an illustrator, marriage to Niamh, possibly children, and a long and happy life all stretched out ahead of him.

Back at the Maitland family home, life carried on much as normal. Iain was still a writer, but was moving away from stuff-and-nonsense articles – 1000 words on putting horse manure on a roof to age tiles was something of a final straw – and was now writing more and more about property matters. Forward contracts, exchange rates – stuff like that. Tracey still worked with small children at the local primary school. By now, Iain and Tracey had been together for close to 35 years.

Sophie was working and playing hard at Durham University on her way to getting a degree in Psychology. She was due to complete her degree the following year but was not sure what to do after that. Adam was coming up to starting his GCSEs. If he did well enough, he would go on to do A Levels. Bernard the dog loved and was loved by everyone – a happy little dog. Indeed, a happy little family.

Life was good – in fact, it couldn't really get much better!

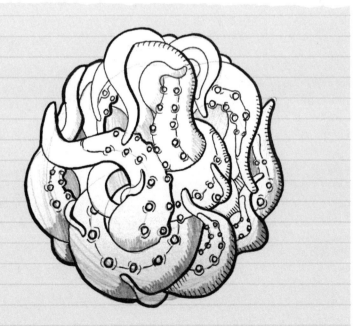

THE THING WITH MENTAL ILL-HEALTH IS THAT HAS MANY TENTACLES AND NEVER REALLY GOES AWAY. IT'S ALWAYS THERE, WAITING...

Part Two

GOING HOME

We continue our story into Part Two with Michael being discharged from the Priory and returning to his home with his girlfriend, Niamh, in Ipswich in Suffolk. He was now only going one way – up, up, up – and relationships with the rest of the family – Dad, Mum, sister Sophie and brother Adam – could be rebuilt over the coming months.

This second part of the book takes us from March 2013 to May 2015, just a few days after the Ipswich v Norwich Championship Play-Off Semi-Final which the Maitlands watched on television as a family. In the same way that Niamh featured in the pivotal moment at the beginning of the book – the 'Is it terminal?' text exchange – so she did again here. Niamh's phone call to Sophie a few nights after the Play-Off Semi-Final, asking for the phone to be passed to Tracey, caused huge excitement in Iain who rushed in to shout, 'Is she pregnant!?' But we get ahead of ourselves...

Michael kept a dairy, on and off, and sometimes just notes, over this time and these reveal what was happening and how he felt over these months and years. As in Part One, entries are broken up to show they were written at different times – days apart this time rather than hours in the Priory, by simply inserting '...' again. The alternating text by Iain documents what was happening to the family alongside Michael's life. There are also more self-help ideas as we go along.

March 2013
I'm out

I got discharged!

I had been waiting for that meeting for so long. Niamh's mum came up to sit in and listen as Niamh was at work. The meeting lasted around half an hour and there were quite a few members of staff there, including the big man himself, Dr Webster.

I had a feeling it might finally be time for me to go. He spoke for ages about how bad I was coming in and how likely it had been that I would die. He said he was shocked when he first heard about me and was worried I could die.

After he spoke for a while, he then let me speak – this is the part where I had to try to not say anything weird and make sure I sounded normal. I had to sound sane! I think I must have done a good job, and when it came to him saying he'd decided to discharge me, I cried a little – or possibly quite a lot.

Dr Webster spoke about me seeing Colm once I got home and having check-ups with him. He also asked me lots of things like what my time here was like. I said I hated every minute of it and laughed, and he laughed too. I think he thought I was joking. He also told me again I was in an awful mess when I came in and he was worried I could have died. I think that's why I ended having to stay a lot longer than I had expected...two weeks!

Niamh's mum then drove me home because Niamh was still at work. I don't think I've ever felt so free as I did on the drive. I didn't know what to think. Imagine being locked away for so long, not seeing friends and only very occasionally seeing family, and then getting released. I think being locked up helped me but also drove me a little bit madder as well. I think it would do that to anyone, being in a situation like that. I know it's changed me. I just need to wait and see what happens from here. It's going to be good.

When I got home, I unpacked my stuff. The sun was shining outside and I felt happy for the first time in what seemed like years. I was waiting for Niamh to get home from work. She came running through the door and gave me a huge hug and cried. It must have been awful to have been here on her own for so long. I think it must have affected her quite badly too, but she would have not wanted me to know that. We talked for the whole evening and were so excited to finally be able to do stuff again. We went for a walk in Christchurch Park and sat on the grass until it got dark. I then cooked dinner for Niamh – something I don't think I've done in years.

* * *

I think being in the Priory did help me but I think it has its flaws as well. I think I needed it; otherwise, I probably would have died. Also, seeing Richard, who did my CBT sessions, helped a lot. Not because of the practical stuff, more just because we became good friends and he was one of the first people I had talked to in a long time, and not just about mental health stuff.

Being in the Priory is weird because it's a place designed to help you get better, but, in my view, being shut away behind locked doors, being forced to eat huge amounts of food and then having to deal with being there 24/7 isn't good for your state of mind.

I did feel at times I was losing it a bit, and at the beginning I did want to make a run for it. I saw it as a game being there. You have to play by the rules, which mainly involves pleasing the staff so they can tick the right boxes. I had to do what they said, be involved and pretend to be normal.

It has changed me. The main thing it made me think is that there's no way on earth I'm ever going back there. I can't go through that again. Imagine sitting in your room being scared of your next weigh-in so you force down a whole packet of custard creams in one go. That's what I think is wrong with the place. Sure, it helps get your weight up, but I think more could be done to help patients' states of mind.

* * *

I need to try to find a way of adjusting back to normal life again – well, as normal as I can be. It's nice finding routines again. I find safety in routine and it helps my mind. I want to try to be more spontaneous if I can, though. I don't want to feel confined. I have to see Colm (my local mentor) for the next few months as he is meant to check up on me and make sure I don't lose it.

I like having some sort of routine. I like to make sure I get out of the house. At weekends, I'm going to make sure I spend the afternoons doing something outside. I'm going to go for walks in Christchurch Park in the evenings with Niamh. I also like going to the cinema on Sundays with Niamh or my family.

* * *

I see Colm once a week and he comes to my house. He weighs me when he sees me. I see him looking around my house when he comes in and he asks things like what did I do this morning, what are my plans and if I'm going to try to see my friends. We just chat really. He tries to keep it fairly casual, like we are just mates, but I can tell he's trying to suss out how I'm feeling.

In a way, seeing Colm is hard because, although he's really very nice, I feel that I know more about mental health than he does, and when he tries to talk to me, I can't help but feel he is reciting theories from a book. He doesn't really understand as he's not been through what I have. That's the trouble. I feel that I can only connect with people and talk about the way I am if they have experienced mental health issues themselves. If you have not experienced depression, how you can advise someone about it?

LET'S TALK MORE ABOUT SELF-CONFIDENCE

In this last diary entry, Michael sounds more confident than he has done for a long time. It's important to work on your self-confidence, though. It's not something to take for granted, especially if you have (or have had) issues with self-esteem. Here are some thoughts you might find helpful.

List some positives

We've touched on this before with 'the list of truths' but it bears developing a little here. It's a useful idea to have a list of 'good things' in your life. Creating a list can reinforce confidence and, as and when things dip, this list can be referred to. I know people who chalk it up on a board in their house (kitchen or bathroom – somewhere they see it regularly) and look at it from time to time, adding new good things as they go along.

You might, perhaps working with a friend, want to list what's good about you, the people you have around you, the things you've done that make you feel positive or others feel happy, and what things people have done for you that make you feel good about yourself. Make this as long a list as possible.

Perhaps someone has paid you a compliment, saying your work was good, completed on schedule, etc. That should go on your list. You may want to update this list regularly as good things happen and carry it with you so you can look at it now and then. Some people rework this idea and have five to ten 'good things' listed on a postcard that they carry with them and look at it from time to time.

Be with upbeat people

If you have people around you who are positive and upbeat and always 'see the bright side' of life, they will help you stay positive. If you have gloomy and downbeat friends who are cynical and always see the worst in everything, it's really hard to avoid that creeping influence. Be with people who'll say nice things – about you too.

Social media has many upsides, but it is often a cesspit of negative views and emotions, with people making comments and loading photos and videos that they would never reveal face-to-face in a family or friends get-together. If you have mental health concerns, you really need to think carefully about your social media activities and how these affect your well-being.

You may want to rethink who you are spending time with; you may need to make some tough choices here for your own good mental health. You don't have to stop seeing people completely; just be aware that those who are negative aren't going to be doing you any favours mental-health-wise. Being with happy people makes it more likely you'll be happy. Say something nice to them – they'll probably say something nice back.

Talk to yourself

When you talk to yourself – as we all do from time to time in our heads (or, as I do, to the dog) – the key is to talk as you would to a loved one, not to someone you don't like.

Michael's internal self-dialogue, as we saw in Part One, has been incredibly self-critical at times and so damaging to his mental health. In essence, he beat himself up mentally day after day, hating the way he looked, how he felt and so on. He destroyed his own confidence.

It's better to try to focus on upbeat thoughts about yourself: 'hair looks nice today', 'my coat suits me', 'I completed that job perfectly – well done me', 'I did Rajesh (work colleague) a favour and that saved time so he could catch an early train for a weekend away', etc.

Stay active

From what we have seen so far, Michael is in a better mental place when he gets the work–life balance right for him. He wanted to be busy-ish, to keep his mind occupied and his thoughts away from darker places, but not so busy and overworked that he became stressed, which impacts on his mental well-being. He, like everyone else, has to get that balance 'just so' for him. (The exact 'just so' is likely to vary for everyone.)

So, for most people, it's important to be active (or at least active-ish), working without pushing themselves too hard, enjoying hobbies and perhaps trying new ones, and taking some physical exercise – it costs nothing to walk or jog or run, except a decent pair of shoes or trainers, and skipping, swimming and cycling are often not that expensive. They can make huge differences to your mental health. It's been said by many experts that 30 minutes of exercise a day is better for you than medication; that's certainly not to say that you should bin your meds – not at all – but it shows the significance of regular exercise.

You need to be aware of your limitations, though – you don't have to run or swim to the point of collapse to prove you can do it – and it's wise to set some boundaries: 'I'll swim for 30 minutes and see how I feel.' It's also good to be able to say 'no' to extra work or overtime if the request is likely to move you from 'being busy' to 'becoming stressed'.

Have goals

It's often helpful to have something to aim for – whether it's like Michael's desire to get back on his master's course and enjoy and complete that or something that's more personal to you. What is it you want to do over the coming weeks, month, year or two?

It does not have to be a 'BIG' goal – to write a novel, to run a marathon – and it can be quite simple – to learn a new skill, to visit a place you haven't been to for ages, to meet new people. It's good to have something in front of you. At various times in his diary in the Priory, Michael expressed sadness that he had nothing to look forward to; having something ahead of you is a boost.

It's also worth mentioning 'small steps' here. There is an old Chinese saying that goes something like 'A journey of a thousand miles begins with a single step'. We could add 'and continues with one single step at a time'. You don't have to be 100 per cent better today, tomorrow or next week – just a tiny little bit at a time. And do celebrate in some way – even if it's only buying some cherries or a bag of sweets – when you reach a goal. Michael, at least to this point, struggled to ever treat himself. It's important that you do.

Other things to do

Talking to parents and young adults with mental health stories to share, I am often offered tips and suggestions by them. Here, in no particular order, just to set you thinking, are some of these ideas that may help you and yours. Remember, with good mental health, there is no one-size-fits-all solution – you have to try different things and see what works for you. Some will work, others won't. It may be a different mix for someone else.

Take care of your appearance. For some, this is almost a 'first things first' tip. They say that to feel better, it helps to look better – so just getting up and washing and wearing clean clothes and brushing hair, simplistic though it all sounds, is a good start. Michael, pre-Priory, spent many days alone in bed, and his mood stayed low and got ever lower. The Priory got their patients up early and got them going. There may be something in that, mental health-wise.

Get to know yourself. Some people with mental health issues talk of an ebb and flow in how they are feeling. They know when they are feeling okay-ish and can tell that a downturn is coming. It's a good idea to try to monitor your moods so that if you know a down moment is on its way, you can prepare for it. One person I know, anticipating a decline, makes a conscious decision to 'keep busy' so that they can work through their low mood more effectively. Others may want to take time out. These approaches work for them but may not be how it works best for you; it's a personal decision.

Be kind. Many of these self-help tips seem simple and obvious and, even better, they work for those people who suggest them – and yet not everyone follows them. Another tip is simply to be kind, to help, to be nice to people – on the basis that they will reciprocate. One of the issues with mental health is that sufferers often become very inward-looking to the point where they can seem self-obsessed. Combine that with the common desire to hide the mental illness from those around them and it becomes clearer why such simple steps are not followed. But a kindness makes both sides feel better and is often returned. It's worth a try for sure.

Stand up straight and speak slowly and smile is, like getting up and getting dressed, another 'first things first' for some people. It also has echoes of what we mentioned in Part One of the book: act in a certain way and that's how you (eventually) become. This tip has the added benefit that it conveys self-confidence, which is always a positive. The word 'smile' or the phrase 'keep smiling' is repeated again and again in these conversations. It was only when I saw Michael smile – really, properly smile – that I realised how long I hadn't seen him smile and that he was getting better.

April 2013
Niamh and me

Niamh and I are getting along well, probably the best we have in a long time. I've known her since I was 18. (We met on a foundation degree course in Art at Suffolk College in Ipswich.) We know each other better than anyone else. We both know what the other is thinking at any time. She is helping me adjust back to life here.

I still feel weird, but free. I want to start drawing again and prepare for going back to finish my master's. I dropped out during the first year of my two-year Moving Image and Sound course, so I will see some people I met who will now be in the second year. I don't know if I'll try to explain where I've been. How do you casually drop into conversation that you've been in a mental asylum for months on end? Tricky one.

* * *

Niamh's dad came round for a coffee and I don't think I've seen him properly in over a year. He's sometimes kind and friendly and others not approachable at all. I still remember the first time I met him at his massive country house. Niamh had an amazing house and was very well-off growing up. Niamh's dad didn't stay long; he never does. He's always dashing off and keeps himself to himself.

WHEN I AM HAPPY I DRAW - I'VE ALWAYS LOVED SKETCHING.

AN ASIDE ON MICHAEL AND NIAMH

This was a promising time for Michael – from our arm's length perspective, it looked as though his life had hit rock-bottom in hospital and at the Priory and he was now going to turn it all around; getting healthier and happier, going back to university and maybe finding a part-time job.

His relationship with Niamh seemed strong and permanent in much the same way as mine and Tracey's was and is. Forever and ever. Indeed, Michael and Niamh talked of getting married in the coming summer. It did seem, at this moment, that everything was going to come good for him, them – and us (at last).

Of course, even at this point in Michael's story, we did not have a great knowledge and understanding of mental health, assuming that it could be 'fixed' and that would be the end of it. How little we knew! The reality is that, for most people, it is part of their ongoing lives for a good while, if not longer. No matter (so we would have thought then) – it could, at the very worst, at least be managed successfully.

A LITTLE BIT MORE ON POSITIVITY

Hard to believe that Michael's last diary entry was written by the same person who only a few months before was having close-to-suicidal thoughts. The key now for Michael, as it is for many who have come back from mental ill-health, is to stay positive. Here are some more suggestions. Again, pick and choose those that seem best suited to you.

Begin the day with a positive affirmation

Some people find it helps to look at themselves in the mirror first thing in the morning and say something like 'Today's going to be awesome'. You can do the same in your head; it works for many. Having a positive start to the day – maybe a shower/breakfast/catch-up-on-the-news routine that suits you – is important too.

Watch out for 'good things'

Instead of focusing on negatives, it's far better to watch out for anything good that happens to you during the day – the sun was shining, a neighbour took in a parcel for you, someone moved out of your way when walking to work, someone else smiled at you, and so on.

Turn negatives around

We don't want to talk about negatives too much here as this is a happy part of the book, but as you look for good things, try to turn any negatives into positives too. Stuck in traffic? Listen to an extra track or two on that CD you have in the car.

Play upbeat music

Listening to happy, cheerful music can affect your mood for the better. Music that you associate with happy times from your past can be especially effective.

Eat healthily

What you eat is your call, of course – Michael was vegetarian at this stage in his life – but it is good to eat regularly and well: vegetables, plenty of nutrients, etc. We can include drink and keeping hydrated here as well. Alcohol is often not helpful for those with mental health issues, especially those on medications.

Change your language

This one works well for some people. They pepper their language with positives – 'Wow', 'Brilliant', 'Awesome'. At the very least, it sends out positives vibes that often come back to you from other people.

Keep happy photos

A variation on that list of truths or list of good things, some people find it helps to stay positive if they have photos of family, friends and pets to look at as and when their mood dips a little.

Think 'What does it matter?'

This is a tip shared by someone who once, like Michael, felt suicidal. When he comes up against what he calls 'a blip' – he misses a bus, is a few minutes late for a meeting – he thinks, 'What does it matter?' It's a kind of mantra. In the grand scheme of things, most blips don't really matter all that much, if at all. The sun will still rise tomorrow morning.

Stay in the present

Few people, with good mental health or not-so-good mental health, stay in the here and now. Instead, they are looking ahead – to what they have to do tonight, next week, the month after or whatever (and dwell overmuch on worries about it). Keeping your thoughts on now and doing what you are doing at the moment and just enjoying the present are helpful for most people.

Get some exercise

Most people benefit from a little bit of exercise regularly, perhaps 20–30 minutes a day of walking or some stretching exercises after work or a gentle yoga wind-down at the end of the day. (I talk about exercise a lot when doing presentations to students and parents and can't repeat this enough – exercise is so great for mental health.)

Wind down the day

In the same way that you can start the day with a positive affirmation, you can, after winding down to bedtime slowly and peacefully, end it in much the same way. Reflect on the good things that happened to you today.

May 2013
Rebuilding my life

I have started applying for jobs again in Ipswich. I'm not sure what to do but thought it was worth a look. I've had a job before, working in a kitchen in a restaurant at Felixstowe, but I want to find something in Ipswich that I can handle. I will have a look in Game and see if they have anything going there.

I haven't spoken to my old friends from school in a long time. I don't really know what they will think of me any more to be honest. My best friends are – were – Toby and Adam, but I haven't really seen them for ages now. They always tried to help me when I was down, contacting me on and off, but I didn't want to know. I didn't want to talk about it. I think maybe I do now, or soon anyway. I'd like to see them.

* * *

Colm has told me that this service he works for is changing soon and he will be leaving. The team and service in Suffolk is moving into new departments or something. I don't know much about it. Colm will have to leave, so I think he's actually going to retire after this.

* * *

I need to be drawing and doing research for when I start my master's again. My course is Moving Image and Sound. It's basically animation/illustration. I have quite a unique style of drawing and haven't really done much animation before. I tend to use a lot of line work mixed with bright neon colours and take ideas from films such as *Coraline, The Nightmare Before Christmas,* a lot of Tim Burton stuff. Games like the *BioShock* series, *Fallout* and *Dead Space* inspire me.

When I was at university last time, some of the artists there were quite traditional and did oil paintings of the sea and landscapes – all very bleak East Anglian stuff. Others went down the graphic design route, with clean-looking vector art – drawings on a PC using a tablet. It will be weird to see some people I know back at university. I think I'll just drive to Norwich or get the train as it's only part-time, two days a week there, and the rest at home in my own time. It starts in October and runs all the way through to the August, I think. I then do another year through to August 2015.

* * *

Niamh hasn't stopped looking at wedding ideas! I'm just going to let her run with it. I think she's thinking about a wedding abroad if she can. I think my dad and her dad will come together to sort it. Niamh has a few places in mind and she wants it to be somewhere hot.

* * *

Niamh has found a really nice place in Antigua with private beaches, all-inclusive food and drinks, and really nice hotel rooms. We will invite just our families to the wedding as it's going to be expensive to get there. Niamh's dad has said that he wants to help with the wedding. Niamh's dealing with that. I think Niamh's family is happy for us, although I never really know what they think about me.

I can't imagine any parent would want their daughter to be with anyone who's been as mentally ill as I have been, but they have never shown it and have always been supportive. I hope they like me, but it's uncomfortable seeing them after what's happened with hospital and the Priory. We are happy, though, and that's what matters.

* * *

Life feels more normal now I'm out of the madhouse. I know I'm still weird and probably will be for ever. I think it's hard not to be a bit crazy after being through rehab and living how I have done for probably six or seven years. I can probably only just count on ten fingers the number of mental health issues I've experienced, from anxiety and depression to OCD. I think I've learned to cope a lot better.

Being home is testing me again a bit, though, because I don't have anyone constantly looking over my shoulder like I did in the Priory.

A QUICK WORD ON BEING HAPPY

Being happy is, for most people, what life is all about. Yet happiness is often quite elusive for many who feel they could be happy if *only* such-and-such would happen.

Michael, locked up in the Priory, realised fairly quickly what made him happy and it was mostly simple stuff like being able to walk in the park or pop to the shops when he wanted. For him, it had nothing to do with money or prestige. It was about getting the basics right and in place. (Thumbs up to Michael for that.)

How to be happy is one of those big, universal questions we all want answered. For some, it is unanswerable. Others have to find their own answers. Here, based on the little we have learned, are a few pointers.

Be accepting

Much has to do with accepting what you have rather than focusing on what you don't have. Too often, people say that they will be happy once they have got that promotion, got that new car, moved to a bigger house and so on. (If they get that promotion or bigger house, happiness always then seems to be dependent on getting to the next level.)

See what you've got

Find the good things – happiness – in what you have already. It is often the little things – a child smiling, a dog rolling excitedly back and forth – that bring moments of happiness. These are the good things that should be on that list of yours.

List what makes you happy

If Michael had listed all the things that made him happy at this stage in his life, now that he was back home with Niamh, he could pretty much use it as a checklist and then go through the points every day. You may be able to do the same.

Change or let go

Change what you can, let go of what you can't. There are things in life you can change – what you want, how you feel – and there are things you cannot – the wants and needs of people you work with, for example. Focus on what you can change; trying to change what you cannot will only make you unhappy. Some people just aren't very nice; best leave them to it.

Be grateful

There's a saying that's been around a while in different forms but it goes something like this: 'I cried because I had no shoes until I met a man who had no feet.' It's a matter of putting things in perspective. As a constant reminder, you may find it helpful to list, at the end of each day, the good things that you have in your life. (Big fan of lists, me! The creation of them can be very soothing and can take your mind off minor niggles and worries.)

June 2013
Managing my issues

Things are going well, but I still think of myself as weird rather than as a normal person. I find all sorts of situations tricky, like meeting new people, and I still get anxious about things. Everyone gets anxious, but it's about understanding that being nervous is part of human nature.

These are the main issues I have had, maybe still have...

Depression

OCD

Anorexia

Anxiety

Stress and panic attacks

Social anxiety phobia

Plus many more!

I've somehow learnt to cope better with all of this and I don't even really know how. If I had to think about it, I think it's that because I've been through a lot of really heavy stuff, most things now don't seem quite as bad.

Also, I used to worry about everything, whether it was going for a meal, seeing people or anything really. Now, after so many times of worrying about something and it then turning out to be okay, I've slowly realised things won't be that bad and people won't judge me.

I've also tried to care a lot less about what people think of me. People have their own issues and stuff going on, so I just try to do what I want to do. To a degree, you have to be selfish in life because when it comes down to it, most people are pretty much just looking out for themselves.

I still see Colm once a week for a chat – i.e. I listen whilst he 'subtly' makes observations. He's a nice enough guy, but it's like another game I have to play to show I am normal and well. When he comes here, I always feel like a child. I don't really like it but I can't just tell him to get lost, much as I want to at times.

* * *

Niamh and I are trying to do more when we have time together, like going to Norwich and visiting different places. We are trying to make the most of the freedom I now have. The main issue I still have is feeling ugly. I have always hated how I look and I still feel uncomfortable now.

Feeling like you hate yourself is a difficult one because you can't just suddenly love yourself. I will never be one of those people that loves themselves or has a massive ego because I'm so used to hating myself. I've only just kind of learned to accept who I am and that's about as far as that will go.

I think to get better at 'liking' yourself you just have to make the most of life, find meaningful relationships and keep yourself busy. I personally think it's about finding some kind of self-worth and purpose in life. Without those things, what do you have to live for?

SOMETHING TO SAY ON OCD

When he was in the Priory, Michael had been told that he had OCD and that it was mild – it showed itself mostly in his need to stick to routines and did not really impact on his life all that much. In fact, until someone at the Priory told him he had it, he did not know. It was something he kept an eye on in these early days back home and it was not a big issue for him – it is for others, though, and is often linked to depression and anxiety.

Obsessive compulsive disorder (OCD) is an anxiety disorder. It comprises two key parts – an obsession and a compulsion. So, someone may have an obsession about food hygiene, for example. The compulsion part would come when they cleaned their cutlery (and related items) over and over and over again. Other common obsessions are along the lines of 'Did I turn the oven off?', 'Did I turn the tap off?', 'Did I lock the front door?' and the compulsion in these cases might be to go back and check (and check and check again).

Michael had what was described by the Priory as low-level OCD and it was something that he could work his way through. He could identify his fears – what lay behind his anxiety and obsession – and then address the compulsive behaviour that dealt, at least for a short while, with those fears. Here's how he did it.

Keep a diary

Try to note when each issue occurs. Taking the 'food hygiene' example just given, it may be every meal and snack time. (Often, OCD is not limited to just one fear, of course – the reality is that 'food hygiene' may be one of many hygiene-related fears, with sufferers not wanting to touch anything that may have germs on it.).

Examine your thoughts

Record your thoughts and feelings as each issue occurs. In terms of our food hygiene example, this might commence with 'I might swallow some germs...make myself feel sick'.

Spot the fixes

Note what you could do to resolve that issue. For example, 'wash the plate and cutlery thoroughly'. In effect, you are listing the compulsive behaviours that you use to try to ease the fears you have.

Rate your worries

Next, once you have a set of situations that you have established over a week or two, try to rate, 1 to 10, how anxious you'd feel if you didn't try to resolve each issue with a compulsive behaviour, 1 being 'a little anxious' and 10 being 'extremely anxious'.

Learn to resist

Try to identify one situation where you think you could resist the urge to use compulsive behaviour. Getting an ice lolly out of the fridge may make you 'a little anxious' (because it's possibly germ-free-ish), so that's something you are more likely to be able to deal with than, say, eating in a café which makes you 'extremely anxious' (as there are germs everywhere).

Tackle that 'little bit anxious' situation, resisting the compulsion attached with it for as long as you can. If possible, try to monitor your anxiety levels, seeing how they ease the longer you hold out (the more often you tackle the same situation – as often as you can – the easier it should get).

Resist some more

When you feel ready, move on to tackle another situation, one that makes you feel a little more anxious, and see if you can handle the next situation without giving in to a compulsion. Again, repeat until you feel better able to manage it before moving on to another situation. A good phrase we've seen and heard many times from those talking about OCD is this: 'The fears get stronger the more you give in and the fears get weaker the more you resist them.'

As an aside, as a loved one or parent, it's a tricky balance dealing with someone struggling with OCD. It's tempting, when faced with a younger person who is doing something you perceive to be 'silly' – such as checking the door is locked many times – to tell them to stop it, to tick them off, to tell them not to be so daft. This does not help matters. It is wiser to be patient and encouraging and see if they can find their own way through.

For more serious cases, it is sensible to take medical advice. A GP may prescribe medication such as antidepressants and tranquillisers. They work for some people. The fact that Michael worked his way out of OCD without taking tablets does not make him better or stronger than someone who goes with medication – just different, that's all. Please always remember, what works for one person may not work so well for another. A GP may also suggest CBT, although the NHS waiting list may be lengthy.

July 2013
Getting on with things

I've decided to get another tattoo. I already have two half sleeves and now I'm going to get a big chest piece. I've been thinking about it for a while and Niamh reckons it's a good idea. I'm trying to do things for myself like making bigger decisions and looking after myself – although it's a weird one getting tattooed because that's me putting myself through actual pain.

I think my inability to make decisions came from my anxiety which came from depression. The trouble is that it's all linked. It's like dominos – as one falls, it can trigger something else. If you're anxious or have trouble with making decisions, even if it's what to do with your time off, it's important to remember whatever you choose is never the wrong choice. Nothing bad can happen from doing what you feel is right at that time.

* * *

I'm trying to do more arty things to stay positive. I find being creative has helped my mental health. Vice versa, I know when I'm really depressed because I don't do any drawing, and things like reading, gaming and going out don't happen any more. I've started doing lino cutting and have also been designing logos. Lino cutting and printing is where you use tools to carve into flat, clay-like sheets and then use rollers to apply ink and make prints of what you carved.

I'm trying to focus on things that I know make me feel better. Going for walks, visiting the cinema and seeing my family. I want to try to get in contact with my friends Toby and Adam again. They made one or two attempts to be friends when I was at my lowest and I just knocked them back. I now feel awkward after all that has happened. How can something like that happen and we don't talk for ages and then I try to see them again? It just feels hard. I know that they will understand and would probably want to see me again, but I have always felt like the weird one. I don't feel that I'll fit in with them anymore.

* * *

I've had toothache for ages now – I need to have a tooth pulled out. They offered to do a root canal but we don't have enough money for it. That's the problem with dropping to six or seven stone and being really unwell – it has all sorts of other physical side effects; it can make your teeth weak, for example.

* * *

I've just been to the dentist and my dad took me. I was in there for over an hour whilst my dad sat in the car. A lady called Zelda - one of my favourite games ever - attempted to pull my tooth out. It shattered midway through so she had to spend the next 40 minutes pulling, digging and scraping away. I then made the mistake of looking at the bowl and seeing tooth and roots and blood everywhere. Horrific - like something out of the film *Hostel*. I staggered out to my dad who seemed to be having a snooze. He said he thought I had been a long time and that he had seen an ambulance go by and wondered whether I might have been in it. He did not seem too worried about it.

* * *

I've got my new tattoo - a big chest piece that took four to five hours. I'm really pleased I got it and it's good that I'm doing positive things that make me feel better. Niamh always says I should try or at least think about getting into tattooing work, but I have no idea where to start.

I have also been making some cut-out craft work, which I saw online. You basically cut and build models of well-known characters like Bender from *Futurama* or the Joker from *Batman*. I started with a couple and before I knew it the old OCD kicked in and I had to make them all. I probably have about 50 so far. My room is now full of them.

My OCD has gone away mostly, with some exceptions like that. It's hard to say what I still do that's OCD-like because who really notices things they do day-to-day? I always like to eat meals at set times. I always watch TV with dinner, go for walks in the same place and things like that. I think I just like having a routine as much as anything else.

CBT - WHAT IT'S ABOUT

Cognitive behavioural therapy is described by the NHS as a 'talking therapy' and it's essentially where a therapist will talk a patient through their issues and, all being well, will change their negative thoughts into more positive ones.

The idea behind CBT is that everything – mental and physical – is linked together and that thinking negatively will mean the sufferer is in an endless downwards spiral: more depression, greater levels of anxiety, stress and so on. Current, rather than past, problems are the focus and are broken down into smaller stages.

Some of the exercises we've covered so far are what we call 'CBT-ish' in that they aim to help you to turn positives into negatives, and these (the list of truths, seeing the silver lining) can prove helpful.

Seeing a therapist, perhaps via the NHS or privately, is for cases that are beyond self-help and this can prove to be effective. There will be a course of treatment of, perhaps, up to 20 sessions lasting between 30 minutes and an hour each, once a week or fortnightly.

Michael's sessions in the Priory included looking at his thoughts and feelings and how these related to his actions – because he was thinking negatively, his actions were equally negative. Michael then worked on turning his thoughts and feelings more positive so that his actions were more positive too, and he then entered an upwards spiral.

August 2013
The wedding approaches

It's not long now until our wedding. We are still not sure who will be coming. My family are and I think Sophie's boyfriend, Paul, will be coming along too. Niamh's dad did say he was going to, but every time Niamh says he needs to book flights he changes the subject. Niamh's mum (her parents are divorced) did originally say that she was going to come, but I also have a feeling that she will pull out.

Niamh has been talking via email with the wedding planner at Bluewater, the resort we are staying at. From the pictures I have seen, it does look amazing – the kind of place you would think of for a dream wedding. Private beach, white sand, clear water and perfect warm weather.

We are having to get stuff sorted now for the wedding. Niamh has been going off to find a dress and I have been sorting out the suit I will wear. I decided to go for cream-coloured trousers, a white shirt, bow tie and braces. I'm going to ask my brother to be my best man and wear the same thing as me. I never really wear anything smart, so it feels weird having to try to put on stuff like that. I like wearing skinny jeans, so I have taken my wedding trousers to be fitted to me.

* * *

Yesterday, Niamh and I, as well as Sophie, Adam and Paul, went off to Norwich for the day. The weather has been so nice and we wanted to get out and about. I always like going back to Norwich. I lived there with Niamh for a few years when we did our degrees and I'm going back soon to restart my master's. I know Norwich really well and have spent a lot of time walking around there. We walked down to where I will be doing my master's. I really like that part of Norwich. It's by the river.

* * *

We've just found out that Niamh's mum isn't coming to the wedding – in fact, none of her family is. It's expensive, I know. Niamh was upset. My family is still coming, though, and Paul, so I'm grateful for that. They are staying in a villa nearby.

* * *

Niamh's sister, Maeve, is going to drive us to the airport tomorrow and I imagine her mum will also come along.

* * *

We have now arrived in Antigua and it's probably one of the hottest places I have been. I've never really been anywhere like this. Our resort is amazing and feels very luxurious, but as soon as you leave the resort and see some of the other places, it can feel quite run down, with loads of stray dogs and homeless people. We have two weeks here. The wedding is halfway through and we then get a week after for the honeymoon.

It's crazy to think how weird my life has been over the last couple of years. I almost died and my body was falling apart. I went to rehab where I was locked away for months and told what to do. I'm now sitting here on a private beach, having unlimited drinks whilst my almost-wife is swimming in the clear blue sea. I think that's a good thing to keep in mind – even at your lowest, your life can change. Mine has. I never thought I would have all of this.

* * *

I'm really loving spending time here. I don't think I've been so relaxed in ages. I literally get to do nothing all day except swim, sleep, draw, eat and repeat. I love the rum. I'm definitely going to sneak some bottles home. I always used to find change really difficult to handle but I'm doing just fine with this. Life can be strange sometimes. Sitting here in the sun compared with sitting in a circle of people with different addictions and mental health issues feels like worlds apart. I guess it is.

I have never really been good with change because I feel like it unsettles me. We have moved house a fair few times and I always feel uncomfortable at first. Everyone in life has their own things, places and routines to make them feel at home and feel safe. I think change is important, though, because it teaches you to adapt to situations.

* * *

I've now gone to stay at my parents' place – a villa overlooking the sea at Darkwood Beach – because it's the day before the wedding. We are going for a meal tonight – Mum, Dad, Adam, Paul and me. Sophie has gone to stay with Niamh.

* * *

We went to a nice restaurant, but I am starting to feel really nervous, to be honest. I'm staying in Adam's room and we will get up tomorrow and go for a drink before getting ready for the wedding. As we drive about the island, Dad keeps stopping to feed homeless dogs he sees with supplies of dog food that he has stacked up in the back of the hired car.

* * *

We stopped at a quirky café on the beach that my folks had checked out a day or two earlier. I think it's run by an English ex-pat. There's no one really about and so we have the place to ourselves. We ordered drinks and my dad suddenly turned to me and uttered the immortal line, 'Are you sure you want to do this?' He then added, 'We can get up and leg it now if you want.'

I'm feeling nervous. It's hard to believe that one minute I was in rehab and now I'm in Antigua about to marry Niamh.

* * *

It's the day after the wedding. If I look back over the last year or so, it's crazy to think I've had probably the worst and best moments of my life so far in those twelve months. Hospital and the Priory to Antigua and Bluewater. I don't know how I could top either really.

The day went really well. The wedding took place on the golden sandy beach with my family and Paul – my dad calls him the halfwit, but we all like him really, including Dad although he pretends not to – sitting on wooden chairs behind me. I stood facing out to sea under an arch made of branches and flowers, waiting for Niamh to come down the wooden stairs behind me with my brother and sister. Sophie was Niamh's maid of honour whilst Adam gave Niamh away and was also my best man. My mum, dad and Paul sat and watched; I think my mum and dad nodded off in the sun.

* * *

We are now enjoying our honeymoon. We get unlimited food at the buffet which is full of everything from fruit, pastas, pizzas, fry-ups, puddings and even more. If there's something you specifically want, the chefs will even make that for you – Niamh asked for dairy-free milkshakes. We just get to chill out on the beach every day, ride jet skis and swim.

I've been drawing lots whilst I've been here. I've done drawings of the beaches and views around us and also some character design work for when I'm back at uni. I think that being creative and listening to music help my mind and enable me to chill out. Anyone suffering with mental illness should try to do something creative. It works for me and I have been feeling a lot better lately. I don't think things could be much better than this really.

A FORETELLING

The boy slumped on to his straw bed in his hut on the edge of the village, exhausted but free. He had fought a long and terrible battle with the tentacled monster that had terrorised him for years. Now he had won at last and he could marry the girl he had given his heart to so long ago. And they could live happily for ever.

As he lay there, he remembered the first time he had seen the monster. He had been walking in the woods for ever such a long time and thought he was all alone as he looked for roots and vegetables to pick for his supper. But he heard a rustle from amongst the trees and, turning, he caught sight of the monster's malevolent eye upon him. The boy hurried back to his hut and did not tell anyone about it.

The next time he went back into the woods to find food, the boy kept a watchful eye out for the monster and listened carefully as he walked, trying to hear if the monster was nearby, moving about. He saw and heard nothing until, as he returned to his village, he heard a slow, slithering noise behind him.

He turned and saw the monster on the path. It was big and wide and green and had ten or more tentacles, each one writhing about as if they were fighting and trying to strangle each other. The boy stared for a long time as the monster and its tentacles slowly became still and then, watching him, started edging forwards. This time, the boy turned and ran as hard and as fast as he could back to the village.

After a while, growing accustomed to seeing the monster, the boy started to ignore it. The monster, who would sit and watch and follow the boy, grew bolder as the days and months passed. It began slithering along a few paces behind, then so close that the boy could feel the swish of the tentacles at his back and, eventually, the monster would wrap all of its tentacles around him as he struggled slowly along the path. The monster would only release the boy back to the village when he promised he would not tell anyone.

This went on for a long while. Every time the boy entered the woods for food, the monster would wrap itself around him, some of its tentacles clinging tight to his arms and legs and others writhing about his face. The monster made the boy feel sick and his head hurt too. Eventually, it made him want to die. But he did not know what to do and he was too frightened and ashamed to tell anyone about it. The monster would release him only when he got back to the edge of the village and repeated his promise not to say anything to anyone.

One day, the boy's sweetheart, seeing how thin and ill the boy was looking, followed him into the woods and saw what was happening. She watched in horror as the monster wrapped its tentacles around the boy, pulling his body in, suffocating and squeezing the life force out of him. She ran back to the village as quickly as she could, calling on every hut, telling them about the monster and asking everyone to fetch their slings and spears to chase the monster away.

The villagers, led by the brave young girl, ran into the woods and found the monster about to devour the boy. They attacked the monster, fighting it off with their slings and spears. Even the small children were there, throwing rocks. The girl passed a spear to the boy who, struggling to his feet, stabbed the monster again and again with all of his might. The monster, close to dying, slithered away and disappeared into the woods.

Now the boy was free and could marry his girl. The village arranged for the wedding to take place the following month. Everyone gathered from all around, including his family from the next village, for the ceremony and the celebrations that would last long into the night and maybe even into the next day. The boy and girl, now married, slipped away at the height of the celebrations to their newly decorated and beautiful hut and they embraced in their love.

The next morning, as happy as he had ever been, the boy rose early as the girl was sleeping and stepped out into the warm sunlight. He gazed around, knowing they had nothing to do all day but relax and be together. Everything was good. Their life was perfect. He was full of joy. The boy stood there for an age, happy in himself and all that he had.

Finally, smiling to himself, he turned to go back into the hut to be with his new wife. As he did, he glanced towards the woods and stopped, a look of horror on his face. He saw that old, familiar malevolent eye watching him. The monster was back. It had never really gone away. Now it was here again, watching and waiting for him. And this time it was going to kill the boy.

September 2013
Back to real life

We are now back home in Ipswich. Niamh will be going back to work soon and I'll have to adjust again to being on my own. I think I will find this hard as I've lost a lot of friends, what with moving about and my mental illness, and I find it difficult to meet new people.

* * *

I spend a lot of time at home on my own, so I'm hoping to find a job, even if it's part-time to help me feel better. I don't think I'm going to see Colm any more. The mental health team in Suffolk is changing and I don't feel like it's helping me anyway.

* * *

Colm is retiring and he did say he could apply for me to see someone else. I think I've come far enough now and don't need it. Plus, I don't want to have to talk about my past for the rest of my life. It's draining and I want to move on.

* * *

For my dad's birthday, my mum suggested I draw a picture of *Doctor Who* to put on his wall in his room; he has loads of *Doctor Who* things in there – it's like a *Doctor Who* Shop. I started off doing a sketch of the Tardis but then my OCD kicked in and I ended up drawing as many *Doctor Who* characters as I could think of. I hope my dad likes it.

MY DAD LOVED IT AND RECOGNISED EVERY CHARACTER IMMEDIATELY.

October 2013

Doing my master's

I'm back at university now doing my master's which feels so-oo weird. I have been getting the train up and having to meet people again. It does make me feel anxious as I'm really not used to being around people. I have bumped into a few people I used to know. I still find it awkward seeing people, even in my home town, because they might be aware I have been in rehab. How do you start a conversation with someone who you perceive to be so mad that they have been locked up for months?

University has changed a lot since I was last here a year ago. There are two buildings opposite each other by the river and the courses in them seem to have swapped sides. And there are new people, but they all seem to be very nice. My tutors know what I have been through and my main tutor is really helpful and patient with me.

I'm going to work really hard this time around on my course and try not to go mental again. I have to admit that being 'normal' feels hard. It's hard to explain. I'm so used to being weird and different from everyone else. I kind of feel like being crazy is who I am and I don't really know who I am without that madness inside of me. It probably sounds odd, but I've been thinking about this every day lately.

* * *

At the weekends, Niamh and I like to go and do stuff and see different places. Today we, and my brother Adam, went to Stonham Barns which is a sort of rural leisure park – Suffolk-style – with an owl sanctuary and shops. Adam's like my best mate really. We get to hang out more now that I'm fairly normal. I can still be weird with Adam. It was a nice day out and I also got a call from Game offering me a trial shift on Saturday. I'm nervous but I think it will be a good thing. I'm not even really doing it for the money, but it helps.

* * *

I just had my first trial shift at Game which went okay. It basically involved being in the shop helping customers that come in to buy and trade games. I had to get used to it pretty quickly, and my anxiety levels were through the roof because I'm not used to being around so many people and being forced to interact with them.

The good thing is that I'm a huge geek and pretty much know exactly what's going on in the gaming industry at all times, so that's a massive help. I think many older people frown on video games, but they have helped me through some very difficult times. I think that I will get a call from Game over the next few days to see if I get the job and, if I do, I will know more about what it involves.

When anxiety levels are high, I think it's important to take a second to chill out and breathe. There are loads of breathing techniques out there which can be tried. I also try to take my mind off things by doing something else, something I enjoy, like sketching. I also try to talk to someone. Just a chat with a friend. Even if it's about something and nothing, like which movies we've seen and which games we've played.

* * *

I have the job at Game and start next week! I'm a little nervous but I know the staff in there pretty well, so that's good. I'm more just nervous about having to deal with customers. I think it will be good for me, though. I haven't been used to talking to lots of people for a long time. I think I will be anxious, but it might help my confidence.

* * *

Last night, we went for my birthday meal. I used to dread going out for meals because I'd rather just stay at home. I can definitely deal with doing stuff like this a lot more now, but I still find it hard because I know that people watch me. It was nice seeing my family and telling them I've got a job. They were pleased, which was nice. Niamh always makes me a cake for my birthday.

I start my new job tomorrow and I have a shift from 10am to 3pm. The hours are fairly good, but I have to balance it with my master's course and making sure the days work out okay. I also have to make sure that I focus on my coursework. I want to make sure I do well this time round.

* * *

Things have been going fairly well since I left the Priory, but there are still times I get down, like everyone does. I just have to try to make sure I stay on top of it. I also think it's important that I don't push myself too much and also try to treat myself properly, which is hard when I've become such a pro at self-punishment. I'm way better at being harsh on myself, which probably sounds odd because you would think why wouldn't you just treat and look after yourself?

I'm going to try to start saving some money when I work at Game for Christmas and I also want to buy the PS4 which comes out soon.

* * *

I just had my first proper shift at Game. It went okay for the most part. I also found out I get pretty good discounts, so that's cool. I had to learn how to use the tills. I served people and helped to give advice on games. It's all pretty straightforward stuff. The hard part is adjusting to being around lots of people again.

When I feel life is getting a bit much, I try to break it down and find times in the day to relax. I think that's very important. I just walk about. I like going to the park.

November 2013
A proper Christmas

Christmas is coming soon and we have asked both of our families if they want to come to ours for Christmas Day. It was more Niamh's idea than mine and I'm not sure how keen everyone is on it, but I don't really mind everyone coming over. At the moment, I'm trying to focus on staying happy with as little stress as possible. I can't imagine Niamh's dad will come. I haven't seen him in months, since just before the wedding.

* * *

Christmas Eve is coming up and we will be doing the usual Christmas panto at the Wolsey where the group of Maitland family weirdos sit in the front row and sing along – well, everyone apart from me and Adam who slide down into our seats trying not to make eye contact. My mum and dad are usually first up to dance, probably to try to embarrass the rest of us.

I don't think Niamh is going to go as she wants to get stuff ready for Christmas Day. That's okay, though, as it means that after the panto I can run around doing my Christmas shopping for her. I'm not very good at being organised; my head's enough of a mess as it is at times and so I try to keep things simple.

* * *

It's Christmas Eve and I just got back from the panto and the cinema. I had a nice time. I wish Niamh had come too, but never mind. I'm a bit nervous about tomorrow. It's not so much even about the food. It's more about being around people who know I have had an issue with food in the past. Things would be so much easier if no one knew and I could then just focus on me and how I will deal with it, without the added stress of being watched. I will try to have a good time, though.

* * *

It's the evening of Christmas Day. Everyone has been here apart from Niamh's dad and older sister, Megan. Dad and Sophie had an argument towards the end of the day about Paul who hadn't come over – my dad was pleased and Sophie wasn't – and Soph ended up having a big old spectacular strop before wearing herself out and falling asleep on our living-room floor. (The less said about that the better.)

* * *

I get a bit of time with Niamh over Christmas and the New Year. I'm not sure what we will do. We never really have much money and it can get quite stressful when we reach the point of running out. I remember one time when we were living in the cottage and in the winter when it was freezing cold. We had no heating and the house was almost unbearable, bearing in mind I was very thin. I remember we drove into town which takes 20 minutes and went to the bank to find we literally had no money left. Something like 74 pence. We had to go back to my car and sell some old DVDs on the back seat so we could buy petrol to get home.

* * *

Niamh is now back at work and I'm on my own again, apart from when I have my shifts at Game. I'm still doing my master's, so I need to focus on that. I've noticed I've started to feel down a few times recently and I am not really sure why. I think it's the fact that I'm not used to being around people, and also going from not having much on to now having a job, being married and doing a master's feels a lot to handle – even if it's not actually too much for a mentally sane person.

CATCHING UP WITH THE MAITLANDS

As we come to the end of 2013 and move into early 2014, Tracey and I were still doing much the same as ever – working with small children and writing nonsense, albeit a better class of nonsense, respectively – and all was well at home with the two of us plus Adam and Bernard the dog.

Adam had now started his GCSEs. He did not really know what he wanted to do after that yet, but hoped to get enough GCSEs to have the choice of going on to do A Levels. Sophie was coming towards the end of her final year at Durham University and was working hard to get the best result she could. She too was not sure what she would do at the end of her degree but expected to move back to Suffolk in mid-2014.

We had begun to discuss concerns about Michael's well-being between ourselves. Michael had come out of the Priory apparently fit and well, or so we thought. But as the months passed and moved towards a year out, Michael was still distant with us and did not seem to be putting on weight or appear to be any happier than he had been in the months and years that had led up to hospitalisation and the Priory.

In some ways, he did seem to be making progress, though. Michael and Niamh had married. That had to be a huge plus. They had a nice place to live near a park in Ipswich. Another plus. Niamh had a full-time job with prospects. One more plus. Michael was working part-time and doing a master's. All big plus points that must outweigh his skinny appearance and downbeat demeanour, surely? And yet.

And yet we had nagging doubts. We were not sure Michael was all right. We could be wrong. We did not know what to do. If Michael was on the mend, albeit slowly, and we said anything – 'Michael, you don't seem to be getting any better' – it would surely be a blow to his morale and to our relationship. So we kept quiet and, as before, we hoped for the best. Yep, here we go again…

February 2014
More work at university

I'm off to Norwich today for my master's. I think I have a few meetings and a lecture to go to. I'm going to get the train, which will inevitably be delayed/ broken down/something wrong as per usual and I'll end up standing in the freezing cold for an hour or so. I'll write again after university today.

* * *

Uni went okay today, but I found out that I have to do a few big presentations this year in front of a lecture hall of people. I'm really not used to that kind of thing and I'm only just starting to get used to being around large groups of people again.

Also, a few people have asked me why I dropped out and I do find it a bit awkward talking to people at the best of times. A guy called Sam came right up to me and asked where I'd disappeared to. I just had to say I hadn't been ready to start a master's last year. He was trying to be friendly, I think. It all made me feel rather uncomfortable, though. I wish people would just leave me alone.

DEALING WITH SOCIAL ANXIETY

We've seen, through comments in his diary in the Priory and his 2013 and 2014 notes, that Michael has an ongoing issue with meeting and mixing with and talking to people. This social anxiety – feeling anxious about one-to-one and one-to-group face-to-face encounters – is common, mental health issues or no mental health issues. Here are some suggestions.

Plan ahead

Whether you are meeting people one-to-one at, say, a business event or party, or you have to talk to a group, perhaps to present your work in some way, you should allow yourself plenty of time to prepare. If Michael had been able to prepare what he was going to say and how he was going to say it at those CPA meetings in the Priory, it might have been a less stressful experience for him. It might not have gone so well that he got discharged on the spot, but it could have avoided the emotions he showed at the time – crying, swearing, etc. He tried to wing it – which adds to the anxiety levels.

Liken it to a play. There's a period of rehearsals and dress rehearsals first so that it goes right on opening night. Miss out the preparations and opening night is going to be really stressful and you're probably going to fluff your lines.

Whatever is happening, you'll probably know roughly what's expected to take place and how it's meant to pan out. At a meeting, you're going to have to smile and say hello, shake hands, make small talk, listen to what other people have to say, make some comments of your own and so on. At a presentation, you're possibly going to have to introduce yourself, talk through a PowerPoint presentation to make your points, conclude, take questions afterwards, etc.

If you can break down each of these events into smaller steps – first, say hello, second, make small talk and so on – it is easier to imagine what you will do at each step. You can prepare by working through each step with a friend or family member. For example, have a few comments ready for small talk: weather, the journey there, mutual friends and colleagues and so on. It's also a good idea to imagine the event unfolding as you want it to, with you saying the right things at the right times (because you have prepared well) – the more you can 'see' it in your head, the easier it becomes.

Analyse your emotions

Before you do whatever it is you're going to do, your preparation should really include looking at and anticipating your thoughts and feelings – your fears really – to analyse them and see how valid they are (and to try to turn them into positives, of course). We're trying to keep the self-help sections upbeat in Part Two of the book and are focusing on positives rather than dwelling on the negatives, but social anxiety is one issue where we need to address negative emotions head-on.

List, as best you can, what it is that makes you feel anxious about this particular situation and then, for each point, ask yourself:

Why am I thinking this (negative) thought?

What alternative thoughts are there?

What is (really) likely to happen?

How important is the outcome?

So, let's take an example. Jumping ahead here to the current day (more of that in Part Three), I talk to small groups and big halls full of students and parents at schools and colleges and to employers and employees in the workplace about our experiences of mental health. It's quite a sad and emotional story in places, and so I try to lighten some of it, especially early on, with a few jokes and even some black humour. Most of it goes down well; one or two comments don't.

A personal example

As I tell our story up to the point where I received that text from Niamh telling me Michael had been taken to hospital, I make one or two jokes. By keeping the start of the talk light-hearted, there is more of a dramatic impact when I read out Niamh's text and my reply. There is usually a collective intake of breath.

One joke is that Michael, when he went to university, changed his hairstyle a lot. Depending on the audience, I then say he went through a range of hairstyles – Donald Trump, Mahatma Gandhi, Princess Leia, Adolf Hitler. It's a fairly basic joke, but it releases any tension in the air and usually gets a decent laugh if I've pitched the right examples to the right audience.

The Adolf Hitler comment, perhaps surprisingly, often gets the biggest laugh, but on one occasion there was a stony silence and it threw me a little and made me anxious because the week before it had gone down very well and there were one or two guffaws (possibly because no one could quite believe I'd said it). The silence this time round worried me and, as I took a sip of water and clicked through the PowerPoint for a second or two, this raced through my mind...

Why am I thinking this negative thought? Because I made a joke and there was silence and it usually goes down well. Do they think I'm crass? Have I been insensitive? Am I stupid? Is it me screwing things up or is it my anxiety taking over and making me overreact to something that's largely something and nothing?

What are the alternatives to the 'I've screwed up' thought? Maybe I just rushed or mumbled the punchline? Perhaps they didn't all hear me – it's a big hall and my microphone isn't working that well. Could it be that it's not their sort of humour? Were some of them waiting for others – the bosses – to laugh? I've made four or five jokes now and some people have laughed at one or two, others at the other ones. You can't win them all.

What is likely to happen next?

What happened next was really down to me. I could stop and become flustered, maybe apologise, and then stumble anxiously through the rest of the presentation without ad-libbing or making any other comments except those in the script. That's a recipe for a flat and dreary speech. Or I could shrug it off as one of those things and complete the rest of the presentation as I normally would with a mix of drama and humour – some funny, some misplaced – which is what I did (and it went well).

How important is the outcome?

I wanted to complete the presentation so that those in the audience knew that if they or their loved ones experience mental illness, they aren't alone, and that by sharing our story and giving them some how-to suggestions and what-to-do thoughts, they could maybe resolve their issues more effectively than we did. I also hoped to see them come up to me afterwards and share their stories so that they engaged with me – and they did on this occasion as they always do.

Anyway, I found out afterwards from talking to the organiser that, microphoned, I was going live to all of the company's offices. I had assumed – poor planning on my part – that the offices were across the UK. They were actually across Europe, including several offices in, um, Germany. The UK audience did not laugh for fear of offending their German colleagues, who were, I was told later, comfortable with the joke.

Climb a social anxiety ladder

What works for some sufferers is writing down all the scenarios that cause them social anxiety and then listing them, a little like a ladder, with the scenario causing the least anxiety at the bottom and the one that causes the most anxiety at the top. At the bottom might be asking someone in the street for directions and at the top might be making a presentation to 200-plus people.

The aim is to try to work through these one at a time, from somewhere near the bottom to somewhere near the top, so that, as you gain experience, you move from socially anxious to socially relaxed. During this time in his life, Michael put himself into situations that made him a little anxious so that he could learn to manage his fears and then, having handled one lower-level situation well, could move towards the next one.

As important as doing your preparation beforehand is completing your homework afterwards: looking back over what happened, breaking it down into smaller steps and seeing what went well and where you could improve. For Michael, and most people, looking back can be encouraging as it's almost always the case that the event went far better than expected. Michael's social anxiety eased when he did the same thing several times – presentations to fellow students about his work – and realised, from each previous event, that nothing really bad ever happened. He fluffed the occasional line and he clicked to the next PowerPoint page too late once or twice. So diddly what? It's no big deal.

Other points to consider

Again, those who have experienced social anxiety offer a range of tips that work for them and may do so for others. Acting 'as if' you are confident – in this case, socially relaxed – can be helpful. Ask yourself what a socially at-ease person would do – and do that. Eventually, acting becomes reality for many people.

Several people have suggested 'staying in the now'. Most people entering a social situation worry about what's next. So they are getting through the introduction and the small talk but, all the time, they are thinking ahead to the next step and what could go wrong. By staying in the present, you are more likely to make a success of the here and now as your mind is not distracted by thoughts of the next stage.

Focusing on the other person is a good tip that works for many. Instead of looking inwards at what you might say and do, possibly wrong, you look and listen to the person you are talking to, asking them questions and listening to their answers. This can be a good way of getting through a one-to-one, encouraging the other person to take the lead, with you reacting rather than acting – always easier to do.

May 2014
Onwards and upwards

We have started thinking about trying to buy our own place. We have always rented and it can be quite a waste of money pouring hundreds a month away like that. It makes way more sense to get a place with a mortgage if it's possible. I think Niamh is going to start looking. She is always in charge of that stuff and most things really. I just go along with whatever. It's weird how I'm like that. I'm so particular with some stuff and then I can be totally laid-back about other things.

I am particular about certain things. I have to have a shower as soon as I get up. I have to have only my favourite types of cereal – Crunchy Nut Cornflakes, Crunchy Nut Clusters or Quaker Oats. I like having specific foods too: vegetable stir fry, vegetable pasta bake, quesadillas. I'm vegetarian. I have to get out of the house at least once a day.

I have to listen to music when I go to sleep. I like routines. I don't like change.

Yet I'm laid-back about other things. I think I'm laid-back when it comes to doing things with Niamh. If there's something she wants to do or somewhere she wants to go, I just go along with it. I'll watch any rubbish programme and I like to think I can be fairly easy-going. I just have my own struggles that I try not to share with other people. I keep them to myself.

* * *

I've still been doing lots of university work. I think I'm going to turn my illustrations into some kind of animation. I know at the very end of the course we have a massive show, so I want to try to make something cool.

My shifts at Game tend to be all over the place. The shifts aren't very long but it can sometimes be dead quiet and really boring. I'd rather it was busy all the time so that time passes quickly.

It's good to have a job, but doing something with no satisfaction or sense of output/achievement is something I find really demoralising. At some point, I need to find a job that lets me do something I like.

* * *

Niamh has been looking at a few houses and she's seen a couple she likes. I nod and agree. She wants to live a bit more out in the countryside whereas I prefer living in the town, but it's not that a big a deal for me.

* * *

I'm thinking about dyeing my hair. I've always changed my hair a lot. It's good to try new things, so I want to bleach my hair as white as possible. I saw a film with Ryan Gosling in called A Place Beyond the Pines – and I thought his hair looked cool. My hair is pitch-black now. My dad says it is the exact same shade as Hitler's was and that I should grow a matching moustache. It's going to be a real mission getting it white.

* * *

From the outside, Niamh and I probably look like we have a pretty perfect set-up. We are married, have been together for years, have family, have a house and jobs. We also argue like any couple. The difference with us is that I've been mental for such a long time. It can make a relationship unbalanced when there's someone with mental health issues, and I have pretty much had the lot. I do feel myself getting down sometimes and it does have an impact on things. It's weird – if I'm down, then most of the time Niamh will pick me up, but sometimes she has had enough and that's when it feels like things are breaking between us.

If you live with or you're in a relationship with someone who suffers with mental health issues, I think it is important that you have patience. I think it's also important that you talk, but not pressure that person. Pressuring or forcing them to do something might make them feel uncomfortable and push them away. People with mental illness just need to know they have people around them so that they can find their way through in their own way when they can, without feeling they are being pushed or pulled in particular directions.

If you're the one suffering with mental health issues, I think you have to make sure you have good people around you who are reliable. I'm lucky I have a good family. I also have two close friends I have known since I was about six, Toby and Adam, who have come back into my life a little bit lately. It's also important to know that you're not alone and there will always be someone you can talk to, not necessarily about illness or how you feel but to just chat generally about movies or anything really.

* * *

Niamh has shown me a house that has just come up for sale. It does look awesome, so we are going to go and look round it on Saturday morning.

* * *

I had university today and travelled to Norwich by car this time. I've been getting fed up with the train delays and it's been a bit cold lately. I've never been good with cold, and to be honest I get a bit nervous now ever since I had pneumonia and my lung collapsed and I ended up in hospital and then the Priory. Even when I breathe now, I can still feel that my left lung feels strange. I think it's better driving up, even if it takes longer. I've started to make friends. I do struggle doing that, as I'm not very good at letting people in.

Letting people in can be difficult if you're suffering. In my case, I didn't want to talk to people or let people see me because I didn't want the attention and I didn't want people to see how bad I was. I think you have to try to put yourself out there, though, even if it makes you uncomfortable at times. I am trying to do that.

* * *

We just went to look round the house for sale. It was an open viewing, so there were quite a few people having a look at it. It's a little cottage with a garden and it would have a studio space for me. As soon as I looked at Niamh's face as we left, I knew she wanted it. So we literally drove to Tesco, pulled up and put in an offer. We now just have to wait to hear back to see if it will be accepted. I know Niamh really wants to move, but I do love our house now near the town centre. The problem is the place we are renting is going to be sold by the landlord, so we would have to move sometime soon anyway.

I've never really been good at dealing with change. I prefer my routines. So moving house, which we have done a lot over the years, is never easy. I would rather just get it over and done with so that I can adjust to a new pattern.

* * *

Just had another shift at Game. I really like the guys I work with, but the stress of balancing the job and university work feels like a lot. Going from not doing much to now being full-on makes it feel a lot more work than it actually is. I also get asked to work midnight launches and my boss keeps putting me down on the rota to work days he knows I'm at university – I think he does it on purpose, to be honest.

* * *

We just heard back from the estate agent and our offer has been accepted! The only trouble is we can't move into the new house for a few months yet. We are going to have to stay with my family for a while. I think we will need to stay a couple of months over the summer. I don't know how much everyone is going to like that. The house is exciting news, but it makes me anxious. I'm an anxious person. I think I always will be. It's change again. I'll need to get back into a new routine that's as much like my current one. I don't like change.

HANDLING CHANGE

Michael has written about change, and the difficulties he has had with it, for some time, both in the Priory and over the past year, as he manages his mental health in his day-to-day life. Change is something that many people struggle with, but there are things you can do to make it a little easier. (We're talking about everyday change here, of course, rather than horrible great heart-rending stuff like a marriage breakdown or the death of a loved one.)

Acknowledge change is natural

Change is a natural part of life, and it's often more frequent when you are younger and you go through school and possibly college and university and different jobs and relationships and places to live. Change happens a lot. It's just the way of things. You have to, as I would say to Michael, 'just crack on with it'. One way or the other, it's inevitable. It's much better if you can go with it rather than resist it.

Change is especially noticeable when you are younger, but there are also changes to come to terms with as you get older – ageing, retirement, downsizing, etc. – although the pace of change may be slower and easier to anticipate and prepare for. When we were younger, Tracey and I lived in a blur of seven houses in seven years – times of constant change. We've been in our current home for 15 years, but one day that will change again and we will be well prepared for it.

One thing to think about, if you are happy with things as they are, is that there must have been changes to your previous circumstances to have got to this position. You might find it helpful to think about where you were, what those changes were and, in particular, how you dealt with them. You would have handled them well enough to get where you are now. Upcoming changes will take you to another place that may be different to what you have now, but it may be better.

Understand resistance is normal

It's a natural human instinct to resist change, especially if you are happy with the ways things are in your life. In some ways, this initial instinct is something close to fear and it's perfectly normal. This instinct has nothing to do with change being 'good' or 'bad'; it's just what it is – a human instinct.

If you've looked back on your previous situation and the changes and the way you handled them to bring you to where you are today, you might want to look forward to see what the changes are and how you might handle them to take you to a new and better place. Change often feels easier to handle if you have some sense of control over it.

Analyse change

Once you have recognised that your first thoughts are most likely instinctive, you can move on to consider change more carefully so that you can take charge of and be an active part of it. You may want to start with a pen and paper to note down what that change is – moving to a new home for example.

You can then list 'what this change means for me', 'how I feel about it', 'the pros and cons' and 'what I'm going to do'. Write down as much or as little as you like – it's your change, after all. You just want to try to get it clear in your head.

As an example related to moving home, you might note under 'what this change means for me' such comments as 'I'll have a bigger bedroom', 'I'll have further to drive to work', 'it's a nicer, quieter area', and so on. As with other lists we've mentioned before, you may want to do this with an upbeat friend so you get a good mix of thoughts in there.

A friend can also help you list comments under 'how I feel about it'. So, 'I'll have further to drive to work' may sound like a negative, but, talked through, you may be able to identify some positives (always a good thing to do) – 'it's a nicer journey', 'there is less traffic on this road', 'I won't have to leave as early'. Most changes have both pros and cons – if you can look at the cons with someone who has more of an independent view, you should be able to find some positives.

OUT OF THE MADHOUSE

When it comes to 'what I'm going to do', you may want to look at ways you can be positive and make the most of change. We talked earlier in Part Two about the fact that there are some things you can control and some things you cannot. It is better to focus on what you can control and, when it comes to change, one thing you can control is how you respond to it. So, when it comes to moving further away from work, a positive response might be that as you can leave later to drive on a quieter road, you can use the extra time to maybe read a newspaper or go for a walk before you leave.

Take charge of change

The more you can get involved with change rather than letting it happen to you, the better you'll feel about it. You may find it helpful to have a plan for dealing with change. So, still focusing on moving to that new home, you may want to break down this 'big change' into small tasks – 'small steps' are always a good way of approaching any 'big journey'.

So a 'to do' list of things that need to be done can help, with tasks being spread out to allow plenty of time. A daily list of 'feel-good' things you can do relating to this change may be helpful as well. So, a move to a new home in the country might involve a different walk each day to find your way about alleyways and lanes, saying hello to anyone you meet, passing the time of day with at least one person on your walk and so on. If you are not so keen on meeting people, you could change some of these feel-good moments to spotting birds or wildlife.

Times of change are always good moments to pay a little extra attention to your physical and mental health. So, physically, getting enough sleep, taking exercise and eating and drinking well are all important. When facing change such as moving home, Michael found it effective to try to stick as close as he could to a regular routine as this soothed him and made him feel more in control. Mentally, you may want to set aside times to relax, do some deep breathing exercises, take a walk and so on.

July 2014
A holiday in sunny Felixstowe

We are moving back to my family home in Felixstowe for a month or two as the lease on our rented home is up and it's going to be a while before we can move into the cottage. We need to now empty our house and clean everything. It's difficult because I love this house a lot. Cleaning it is going to be a mission. We will have to put stuff into storage at my parents' house and at Niamh's sister's place.

* * *

I've decided to quit Game. I know everyone will be really disappointed in me, but it's been stressing me out and I feel like a lot is piling up on top of me. Uni work is increasing and I have to prepare a lot more for shows and lectures. I know everyone will assume I've quit because I'm not well again, but I'm actually trying to look after myself before I get so stressed that I make myself ill. In my head at least, I'm trying to manage my health better, even though I haven't been feeling that great recently.

* * *

We have started moving out a few bits and pieces from the house, but I'm starting to think that there is going to be way more to do than we even thought. It will be nice to be by the sea for the summer and I will be able to do more stuff with my brother and sister, which is cool. My brother tends to come along to the cinema with us whenever we go.

* * *

We have just taken some of our stuff to Felixstowe so we can get a little settled here. We are squashed into a small room, but at least we have somewhere for the time being. We could maybe have stayed at Niamh's mum's place, but I think that would have done my head in one way or the other. Her mum is lovely but I would not want to live with her.

* * *

Niamh and I took Bernard (the family Jack Russell) for a walk along the beach, which was nice. Bernard was originally Niamh's dog and I can still remember meeting him for the first time at Niamh's big house. They had three dogs; Bernard was the smallest. The other two were massive, and when I first walked in and they ran at me, I almost fell back out the door.

That's also when I met the rest of Niamh's family. I drove over to their house to pick her up to go off to our friend's house party. I remember tuning into her driveway with a moat and, at the end, a massive mansion house. I felt out of place straightaway as

I had long bleached hair and pierced ears. I walked in and saw Niamh's dad for the first time. He strode up to me and shook my hand fiercely and then went back to his fire. I then met Niamh's mum who hugged me. Her mum's really nice.

* * *

Niamh is back at work and I'm in Felixstowe at my parents' house. I just got back from a day in Norwich doing university work. There is quite a lot to do now, but the tutors are awesome and help me out loads. I'm doing some cool work that involves turning my illustrations into animations.

* * *

Things are moving forward with our house and it looks like we will be moving there soon. That will be a mission again, though – moving all of our stuff there.

* * *

Things have been stressful for Niamh at work. I have been a little bit down lately as well because I haven't seen friends all that much since I got out of rehab. I've found it too hard to see old friends again regularly. I still feel a bit ashamed, to be honest.

* * *

I've started doing a little bit of freelance illustration via the internet. It really doesn't pay much at all and my dad says I am selling myself short, but I'm definitely enjoying doing more artwork and it's cool getting good feedback from people. I need to start putting together a presentation that I will be giving later on in my university course. That scares me a bit as it will be in front of a couple of hundred people. My animation is also coming together nicely and I'm learning some interesting new skills.

I'VE ALWAYS ENJOYED DRAWING AND DOING CARTOON CHARACTERS OF MY OWN.

* * *

I have noticed my mood slipping a bit lately and I'm not really sure why. I have been on and off different pills for many years. The first time I tried them was when I came back to live in Ipswich and I felt awful. I then tried coming off them every six months but hated how I changed. I think pills are a good way of helping someone in a desperate situation but, in general, I think it's better to find other methods so you don't have to rely on a pill to make you happy.

> I decided a while back that I don't want to have to rely on pills to be happy. More often than not, they made me feel worse anyway. You have to be careful when it comes to antidepressants. You're meant to come off them gradually, whereas one day I lob them all in the bin and the next day I feel like death.

AN IMPORTANT POINT ON MEDICATION

Those experiencing mental health issues such as anxiety and depression, and a whole host of related matters, will, at some stage, hopefully seek help, most likely from their GP to start with. We'll talk more about getting help, GPs, self-help groups and other formal and informal routes to recovery in Part Three of the book.

But, as a general guide, the earlier help is sought, the better. GPs are a good place to start. Michael had issues with some GPs who he felt did not seem to engage with him and he also believed that too many issued pills as a quick fix. Other sufferers have had more positive experiences and these days, with mental health much more out in the open than it was, many GP practices are more on the ball.

Medication is often one of the first treatments offered by GPs and tried by those with mental health issues. Medication works for some but it is not always for everyone. There is no one-cure-suits-all solution to mental health and you have to see what works best for you, but, if prescribed by a GP, medication is worth trying in the first instance, with the correct dosages taken regularly at the right times and for the prescribed period. It often takes six to eight weeks for medication to start working well, so you need to stick with it.

Regular reviews are advisable. Few people with mental health issues want to be on medication indefinitely and often seek alternative ways of managing their mental health, perhaps alongside lower dosages of medication.

Michael did not want to take medication and came on and off the pills for some time, with sudden stops having various physical and mental side effects. Physically, he experienced headaches, constant sweating, muscle pain and tiredness. Mentally, he felt he became more emotional, extremely depressed and, at times, suicidal.

Other people who have come off medication too quickly report a range of side effects including the most common ones of head pains, stomach upsets, dizziness, flu-like symptoms and insomnia, as well as increased levels of anxiety, vivid dreams and increased levels of depression.

If you are on medication and want to come off, it's best to take advice from your GP before you do. They know your physical and mental history, the medication you are taking and the dosages and side effects. Generally, it's wise to come off medication slowly. For example, you might want ease off over two weeks if you have been taking medication for up to eight weeks. Longer than eight weeks, and you may want to taper down over the next six weeks. Check with your GP first.

It may be helpful to keep a diary showing what you are taking and when and how you feel over that time. You can then share this with your GP who may suggest reducing or increasing dosages accordingly. You should also keep an eye on and a written note of your mental health as you come off medication. It can take a month or two for the medication's effects to work through your system. You may want to make sure you have a healthy routine and step up your stress-related and relaxation exercises during this time. Get support not only from your GP but from positive friends and family members too.

A good analogy we've come across for coming off medication is that of trying to land a plane – maybe a glider if you've not been on them very long, a jumbo jet if you've been on them for ages. You don't want to come down from 30,000 feet to the runway in a nose dive. You want to circle for a while, talk to the control tower, get yourself well briefed and ready, and then come down slowly so that you land smoothly rather than crash-land.

October 2014
Home sweet home

We are now in our new home! It's in a village just outside Ipswich. This morning, my dad helped fill up my car and his, and we moved the stuff over in a couple of trips. It's about ten miles between the two houses so it took a while.

We have been putting the place together and making it feel homely. I have a great studio space. I haven't got a proper desk at the moment, but the plan is to go to IKEA at some point and get one and anything else we need to fit the house out.

I'm not very good with change, so I need to get settled here. It's really nice having a garden and the area around us is pretty quiet. I'm used to living in the town centre, within walking distance of shops, not sheep, so it feels weird being further away from that. The house gives me good space to do my artwork. I need to try to do some more art really because it helps my mind and keeps me staying positive.

* * *

We have been here for a few days now and getting more settled. We live much closer to Niamh's work; she can get there in under ten minutes. Niamh has already made friends with a woman who lives close by called Jenna. Her boyfriend is away in the forces, I think, so she's on her own a lot of the time. It's weird to think I'm now married and have my own house. Despite having some bad setbacks, things have fallen into place.

Niamh's mum is popping over later to have a look around the house. I have always been quite close to Niamh's mum and she has tried to help me a lot. She means well. I like her a lot. I also think Niamh is inviting over her friends this Friday night. I knew one of them back when we were at college. I think I'll just find it awkward, though, sitting around having a meal with people I don't really know. Also, they will look around the house and see my weird collection of toys and paintings.

* * *

Last night went fairly well. I do tend to go into my shell a bit around people I don't really know. That can be a problem as people just think I'm being rude, which isn't the case - well, most of the time. It turned out that Jenna's boyfriend is also a bit of a geek and has his own collection of weird man-child things. To be honest, I think most men do. My dad's room is full of *Doctor Who* posters and figurines and he's in his fifties. He also had a blow-up Dalek at one point.

AN ASIDE ABOUT ROUTINE

Michael's routine at this time was very important to him and his fear of change was as much to do with disturbing his routine as anything else. Those with mental health issues often benefit from having a structure to their days. It provides comfort and can reduce stress levels and anxiety. These are some of the common features of a good mental health routine. As ever, it's not set in stone; pick and choose those bits that suit you best.

A regular wake-up time

Most people benefit from getting up at the same sort of time every day, making sure they allow enough time to do whatever they need to do before they have to get to college or start work. If you don't have anything to get up for, it's still good, mental health-wise, to try to be up at a particular time, perhaps to go for a walk or swim. Michael, at his lowest, spent all day in bed, dwelling on his worries, and this was a likely contributory factor in his decline.

Showering and dressing

Some of those who have had mental health issues say that a key part of their routine is to shower and put on clean clothes – something that is natural to many people but one of the first things that gets overlooked when someone is in mental decline. Michael used to spend days and days in bed. Personal hygiene was not a high priority.

A healthy breakfast

All sorts of health experts say that breakfast is the most important meal of the day and something healthy such as porridge offers a good start. Michael did not eat breakfast for years and it was another factor in not feeling good, both physically and mentally. Eating and drinking regularly and healthily through the day are key components of a good mental health routine.

A little exercise

It's good to get some exercise every day, even if it's walking the dog or going to the shops on foot rather than by car. Cycling, swimming or even a little jogging for 20–30 minutes a day does wonders for your physical health and improves mental health by easing stress and tension.

Keep busy-ish

Too much work can make you stressed and anxious. Equally, too little work can have the same effect. You need to handle your workload, perhaps by having a 'to-do' list of things that need to be done today, this week, this month, and then spreading those out according to their priority. If you have too little to do, perhaps because you are unemployed, you may want to fill your day with a mix of activities – gaming, going for a walk, playing on your mobile, doing some household chores – so that you keep busy-ish and your mind is occupied.

A little fun and relaxation

It's a good idea to have some fun in your day, whatever 'fun' is for you – kicking a ball about, singing to music, putting your pants on your head and dancing or whatever. You should build in times when you can relax, perhaps before, during and after work. This might be a mix of relaxation exercises such as meditating on a mantra or doing the eternal flame exercise.

Taking meds regularly

If you are on medication, it's important to follow your GP's instructions about taking them; you may benefit from taking them at regular times, partly because it's easier to remember to do so but also to make sure they work effectively (they may, for example, need to be taken so many hours apart). Michael regularly went on and off tablets cold turkey without taking medical advice and it was detrimental to his physical and mental health.

A regular bedtime

As with a regular wake-up time, most people benefit from going to bed at the same sort of time each night and getting 'a good night's sleep'. Generally, the old 'eight hours sleep a night' maxim that's usually offered by experts holds true for most people. You may want to lead into this by doing some wind-down exercises, such as deep breathing, and avoiding anything that might wake you up – spicy food, fizzy drinks, horror movies, etc.

For most people with mental health issues, a routine is good for them – it offers control, structure, comfort, reassurance and all sorts of mental health boosters. If you're having a stressful journey home, delayed on the train or in traffic, the thought of a relaxing bath on arrival can be a big plus. Of course, it's important that you don't become a slave to it; if your day is disrupted and you cannot do, say, a relaxation exercise as planned, you can still aim to maybe build in the favourite parts of your daily routine, just a little later.

November 2014
Uni's going well

It's starting to get colder again and I know we will feel it here a lot. We don't have central heating but we do have a fireplace. I think we will borrow some electric heaters from my parents. Niamh has been very busy at work. I miss getting to spend time with her, but I also like being on my own, although when I am on my own, I overthink everything and that can sometimes pull me down.

Today I had university so I drove up to Norwich. They have some cool shops there so, after I'd finished, I had a quick look round town and picked up some veggie bits for dinner. I have been vegetarian for quite a long time now and Niamh has been pushing the vegan thing as well. We are giving it a go after I watched some pretty horrific documentaries about animals being mistreated. Trying this vegan thing is hard, though. I just leave Niamh to sort out what we can eat.

I have started putting together my final animation for this year and a small presentation I have to give. My main tutor, Sara, has helped me so much, as well as Raj, my other tutor. I do feel like I'm learning some new skills and that I'm achieving something. Niamh keeps reminding me that having a master's under my belt would be awesome and something not many people get to do or achieve.

Crazy to think I came out of rehab, got married, got a house and will have a master's next year. When you put your mind and effort into something, you can gain a lot. I have also found you have to put yourself in situations you find uncomfortable in order to progress. When I shut myself away and hide from the world, I get worse, but when I do things and meet people, my life improves. Even if at the present moment I'm very anxious.

I still get anxious about things that any normal person would be scared about, like giving presentations to large groups of people. I still find myself getting anxious when I meet new people, and also meals because I know people are watching me because of the anorexia. I try to control my anxiety in different ways. For me, breathing techniques are important and I always take a moment to breathe in and out for a minute or two whenever I feel particularly stressed out.

I also learnt about something in CBT at rehab called decatastrophising, or decatastrophisation, which is about how we can retrain our thought patterns when we are feeling anxious. When I am anxious, I imagine what could go wrong and work out the very worst that could happen (i.e. something catastrophic). To deal with that, I try to think about things I have been anxious about in the past and then think about how it was after the event happened. Often, there's a big difference between the 'bad' expectation and the 'good' reality.

A simple version of this is to think 'what if?' and 'what then?' So, 'what if the worst thing happens, what then?' The worst thing that might happen when I meet someone for the first time is that I could say the wrong thing or dry up and/or go red. What happens then? Not a lot really when all's said and done. They'd probably think I was maybe shy or nervous or, perhaps, weird (which I am). So that's not so bad. It's not like my trousers have caught fire or my head's fallen off.

I also keep a notebook and write down things that I'm anxious about and then afterwards I make a note of how it actually was. That way, I can see my worrying is often not valid. Notes and lists and checklists and diaries are all ways that I try to separate myself from my thoughts and feelings to make sense of them from a distance. I'm not sure that's logical and I don't know if anyone else does it, but it helps me.

THIS IS ONE OF MY FAVOURITE PIECES AND EVERYONE
AT MY PRESENTATION SEEMED TO LIKE IT.

December 2014

Our first Christmas in a proper home

It's coming up to Christmas time and Niamh and I are going to have our first proper Christmas together in our new home. I think we will then go and see my family on Boxing Day. I'll also do the traditional Christmas Eve with my family (the panto-and-cinema combo, mixed with me running around buying last-minute presents).

I have been writing and making video game reviews for a website for a month or two, but it seems to be building up a bit. Another site has contacted me, asking if I want to start doing some writing for them, which is exciting. It means I will be sent games to review and then I post my comments for people to read online. I'll probably end up like my dad, sitting in a room all day, writing. I think my dad's fine with his own company for most of the time, but I am not sure I could do it forever as he does. I think I would go mad (madder anyway).

I think there may also be the chance to make some video content, which is exciting. I have always loved playing games, even though some people think it's bad for you. I have always believed in doing what makes you happy, and when I'm down, playing a game for an hour can take me away from other thoughts or feelings I'm having. I believe playing video games for a period of time can help with depression. I am a bit OCD-ish, though, so I try to limit myself to a set time for gaming; it can be addictive and not so good for you if you have that type of personality. Addiction is the one thing I don't seem to have had – yet anyway.

* * *

Niamh is seeing friends tonight for a party with work. I always find this difficult because I've pretty much lost all of my friends and still get very lonely. I probably spend 80–90 per cent of my life on my own. I don't think being alone helps my mind. I've been feeling down, but no way near as bad as before the Priory. I just have little dips and my eating has been okay on the whole. It's not an issue for me any more. It's just the depression that comes and goes from time to time.

Coming off meds suddenly again has messed with my head. I came off them some time ago and then tried them again for a while, but I've decided I'm never taking them again. I know it's not normal to cry for no reason, though. I still feel guilty when I get down. People always say to me, 'Why do you feel sad when you are lucky and have such a nice life?' I don't know what to say, but all I know is that I'm very lonely and I end up feeling lost.

* * *

Niamh and I have been putting Christmas decorations up around the house. Niamh is fairly stressed at the moment as I think her boss is giving her grief. She doesn't have an easy job and I know that she pretty much has to run things at work. Niamh's closest friend there is also leaving to have a baby soon, so that will put more pressure on her. I can see that she is getting down and finding it too much. I'm trying to suppress my feelings when I'm sad, which probably isn't a good thing, but I don't want to make things harder for her.

Relationships are weird and a delicate balance. People come together and when it works those people would do anything for each other. That's when people truly love each other. Relationships that last are because people help and care for each other and aren't out for themselves. Relationships break, I believe, when there is an imbalance, which is difficult because I believe all relationships aren't always equal. I don't think ours is.

* * *

I've just got back from Christmas Eve with my family. I started by meeting them at the panto, which is always awkward/funny as my brother and I avoid having to sing or dance at all costs, whereas everyone else jumps about and claps and sings along. My mum's the worst. I think she'd lead a conga if she could.

After that, I had to run around the shops grabbing last-minute presents before meeting my dad, sister and brother at the cinema to see the latest *Night at the Museum* film. We have always gone to the cinema on Christmas Eve. I've only ever missed one – when I was in the Priory – and can still remember the first time me and my dad went when I was very little. We saw *Homeward Bound* at the cinema in Felixstowe. My dad remembers the original (*The Incredible Journey*).

I still love Christmas Eve and it is probably one of my favourite days of the year. I got back home and had dinner with Niamh. Tomorrow, we will get up and probably go for a walk in the morning before Niamh cooks lunch.

* * *

Our Christmas lunch was awesome. Niamh made loads of veggie dishes and I love roast veg – I'm stuffed. I'm now just slobbed out on the sofa watching TV, and I think there was talk of my sister popping over for a bit. Soph is still with Paul and I think things are going well for them. I think tomorrow Niamh and I will go into town for the sales before going over to see my family. I always like going there at Christmas time.

* * *

Heading off to see my family now. Had a nice day so far. Boxing Day is always a weird one and over the past few years they have been a bit all over the place. My dad always makes home-made Christmas crackers with scratchcards in them. Sophie or I always seem to win something, which is brilliant. I just wish I could swap all the luck I have in life for happiness. I think that happiness is the key to life and I'd give up almost anything for that.

A QUIET WORD ON LONELINESS

Michael has written about feeling lonely for some time – first in the Priory, where he was surrounded by people, and lately when he was at home with Niamh and was seeing family and friends occasionally and mixing regularly with students on his master's course. How could he be lonely? Hard to believe, but he clearly was. It's all to do with depression again. Here are some thoughts…

Understanding loneliness

Loneliness can, in the most rough and ready, simplistic textbook way, be divided into different types. One is where someone is alone for some reason – what we might call 'proper alone'. Perhaps they have been living with a partner who has died and they are now on their own after many years.

Maybe they have moved away to work somewhere else, far from family and close friends, and they too are alone. That type of loneliness is familiar to everyone – the image of an 80-year-old widow who never sees anyone except when she goes to the local shops is a common, and poignant, one.

Another type is linked with depression. Remember, depression shows itself in many ways – we always describe mental ill-health as a tentacled monster – and Michael became anorexic as a consequence of depression and a desire to gain control of something – anything – even what he ate. Loneliness is a common consequence of depression. Loneliness is almost a state of mind; people can be with friends or in a crowd and they can still feel as if they are detached and alone. Michael's diary entries show that loneliness is a thread that runs through his life. It wasn't, as often as not, that people weren't around. He just felt apart from everyone.

Make a plan

With loneliness (and this applies to different types, although we are talking here about depression-related loneliness), it is a good idea to make a plan for combating it. Michael has often talked of keeping his mind busy to stop it from dwelling on downbeat issues, such as loneliness, and planning ways to 'keep busy' is helpful; routines, schedules, eating regularly and well, exercising at the same sorts of times each day – these are all beneficial.

This 'keeping busy' can be anything from taking up a hobby with people who have similar interests – so there is some common ground and a feeling of attachment rather than detachment – to volunteering; staying busy-ish with people you can identify with is the key. As time passed,

Michael played games online with other people and that seemed to help him.

Be aware of social media

Social media have many pluses but, as mentioned in Part One, they have their downside, what with trolls and anonymity and vulnerable people with mental health issues. It's a potent mix of possible negativity, and those with a depressive and anxious side need to think carefully about their usage of social media.

With loneliness, social media can offer ways to interact with like-minded people and some sufferers have said this is a big plus for them. Michael has benefited from it. You can, for example, find online forums on whatever interests you and can follow what's happening without joining in until you feel ready. That 'being part of a group', but without being pressured to step forward and take the lead, can be a boost.

Many experts say that, generally, with loneliness, it is more productive to try to build friendships that are real and living and active – you see someone face to face, to have a drink and a chat – rather than virtual friendships that can be turned on and off with the click of a button. Building in time to see people – even if it's only to pass the time of day – can be effective. Again, you might join a group – book reading, a writing group – and sit at the back until you feel ready to participate more.

Just do something (anything!)

Those who live with depression, anxiety and related issues often turn away from loved ones and that tends to worsen feelings of loneliness. If you are aware that this is an issue, the trick – often easier said than done, of course – is to try to do something to engage with other people.

It doesn't need to be a big step – remember, we are big fans of small steps here. It could simply be that you'd start with a 'How are you doing?' email to someone you have not seen for years, a smile and a 'good morning' to someone you pass on the stairs or in the corridor at work.

Talk to someone

'Feeling lonely' when you suffer from depression or anxiety is often, at least in part, as much about feeling as though you are different, not understood or uncared for as it is to do with 'being alone'. Michael has often spoken about being 'the weird one' of the family, although, in many ways, it is a self-imposed title.

You can perhaps talk to people who you might perceive to be 'different' too; taking Michael as an example, he has tattoos, quite commonplace these days, and it is relatively easy to strike up conversations with others who have them. That 'difference' then starts to ease away. If I want to strike up a conversation with someone at a seminar or convention and they have tattoos, a simple 'I like your tattoos' is a perfect ice-breaker.

Friends and family, although they may not understand your thought processes, will benefit from hearing them, and spending time together may show that you are cared for. There are all sorts of self-help groups out there too – more on these in Part Three. Who better to understand someone with, say, depression or an eating disorder than someone else who has experienced it?

Other ideas about loneliness

Remember, we always stress that there is no one-size-fits-all remedy and those who have experienced depression-related loneliness offer different ideas. Some may suit you, some won't. You have to find your own way. Keeping a diary – what you feel, when, how long – is suggested by many; this can be useful as you can start to head off anticipated upcoming feelings by keeping busy.

Keep expectations realistic. This touches a little on 'small steps'. In essence, don't expect too much too soon. If you are feeling 0/10 lonely today – and some people have suggested scoring your feelings in this way – you are not going to go to 10/10 any time soon. But a sunny day and some good news in the morning may see tomorrow get a 1/10 score. Equally, if you join a group, you are most likely not going to find a life-long friend or the love of your life (well, you might, one day…), but you may spend time in good company and forget your troubles for an hour or two.

Another idea offered by some is to be as pleasant as you can to people. Many people with depression and anxiety are not fun to be around. Deep breath… Michael was not, over these years, someone who I really wanted to spend much time with except out of parental duty. Let's speak up for family and friends here – it's not easy for loved ones either when they are faced with someone who is unhappy. The more you can engage with people and be positive towards them, the more that comes back your way.

Meditation – we talked of this in Part One – is something that is mentioned by sufferers time and again. Sitting quietly, focusing on a candle, relaxing and possibly chanting a mantra can bring a sense of inner peace and acceptance. Try it – see what works best for you.

January 2015
Life goes on (and on)

Niamh is back at work now and I'm on my own. It's okay because I've got lots of work to be getting on with. It just feels weird at first, adjusting back to being alone again. I don't find it easy, but I'm still working on my series of animations that will all come together at some point. That helps. If I didn't have stuff to keep me busy, I might struggle more than I do. I think I might be in trouble.

February 2015
Days of reflection

Today, Niamh and I went to London for the day. For Christmas, my parents got me tickets to go and see an exhibition by an artist who makes massive Lego sculptures. It was great and nice for us to do something different. I'm not a huge fan of London itself because it's noisy and crowded and rushed, and that stresses me out quite a lot, but I did have a nice day and we spent some time together and we got to chat.

* * *

With relationships, I think it's important not to get stuck in a rut. It's just difficult sometimes with our situation, with Niamh working all the time. She gets back late and is often knackered, and I'm a bit back and forward, so we only get the weekends together and by that time we just want to chill at home. I also like routine.

On a Saturday, we tend to wake up, have breakfast, have baths and get ready. We then go to do the weekly shop at Tesco before coming back home. Sometimes, we stop off at Niamh's work to sort bits for the next week. Then, usually in the afternoon, Niamh will do stuff about the house or we will go into town to look around the shops and have a drink. We then come home and have dinner.

I know it's a pretty simple routine but I like having it. I think in some ways a routine can help someone with mental illness, but I also think it's important to push yourself into trying new things and getting out there. It is not always easy to get it right.

* * *

I'm trying to focus on my work, but my mind has been finding it hard and I'm not really sure why. We have been a bit distant since we got back from London and I'm not sure what to do. I think that we are both just stressed. I need to keep going with my work and make sure that I keep hitting the deadlines. I think I'm doing fine and the tutors seem happy with the work I'm producing. I'm also just trying to make sure that my mood doesn't dip too much. I know I have blips sometimes and it's just about staying on top of it.

March 2015

Down in the dumps

I'm just focusing on my university work at the moment, but I definitely don't feel right. I hope it will just be a phase. These feelings do tend to come and go with me. When that happens, I just try to strip my life right down to the basics to avoid stress. That can be difficult, though, when there's lots on with university.

Niamh is really busy at work at the moment, so we don't see each other a huge amount. She keeps working late and talks about her boss being a pain. I think he just tends to disappear some days or not even turn up.

Niamh is pretty much running things now that her best friend has been on maternity leave and has had her baby. I think her friend wants us to look after the baby at some point whilst she gets some stuff done.

* * *

I just gave a big presentation at university in front of a lecture hall full of people. I had to talk about myself, my work and how I came to make the piece I'm currently working on. My illustration is quite weird and a few people asked me if I was on drugs whilst making it. (No.)

I do tend to make quite psychedelic artwork with bright neon colours. I'm also making illustrations based on the classic Greek myth about Icarus who flew too close to the sun. But I'm doing it set in the distant future with a sci-fi setting. It's all a bit mental really, probably is *very* mental.

I got good feedback, though, from my talk, which was good considering I was a sweaty mess. It was a right nightmare getting home as well. I got the train up and the winds were bad. EVERY SINGLE train was cancelled on the way home. Niamh had to drive all the way up from Ipswich to Norwich to get me after work. I just sat in Morrison's café bored out of my brains.

* * *

I've had a week off university because it's non-taught week. It's nice to just do some work at home, although it's a lot lonelier. I can go sometimes without seeing anyone for a very long time, especially if Niamh has things on and is out in the evenings.

I sometimes do not talk to anyone for literally three or four days. I don't think it's good for my mind and it makes me feel down.

It makes me miss Niamh more and I tell her that, but she is not all that happy about it. I'm reaching out to Niamh because – imagine not having anywhere to be, with anxiety levels rising. If you're not talking to anyone, then you start to think a lot more and it gets worse and worse.

I'll focus on doing some painting and see if I can get any freelance illustration pieces on the go. I've also been doing some more game reviews and have been asked to do a voiceover review for the new *Witcher* game. I do like seeing my work being published on the gaming website and seeing the feedback it gets. I like writing.

* * *

Starting to feel a bit low again. My eating has been okay still and I'm trying not to let my mood dictate that. I just need to keep working and then also try to enjoy the things I like. I'm trying to get out and about as much as I can but I have felt my mood slipping.

Niamh has been staying behind late at work to help out. She mentioned there is a new work colleague there. She is helping him settle in. We have been fairly distant recently and have only been spending a couple of hours here and there together. We used to spend so much time together doing stuff. Every moment we could, really.

May 2015
The end of the world

My heart is broken.

Literally feel in so much pain.

Niamh came home today after work and told me to leave for good.

She wants a divorce and for me to move out.

I feel completely and utterly broken and don't know what to do.

I want to die.

ANOTHER FORETELLING

The boy, with the monster on his back and its tentacles wrapped around him, writhing and twisting at his body, struggled along the path through the woods. He had been walking like this for ever such a long time, at first not noticing that the monster had come back and was behind him, and then hardly realising it had climbed onto his back and had wrapped itself around him again, just like it used to do. Now he knew, at last, that it was close to overpowering and killing him.

He thought that if he could only make it through the woods and back onto the plain and into the safety of their hut, his sweetheart – now his wife – would help him and they could somehow fight off the monster together. If he could just shake the monster off his back and then turn and confront it, they could be rid of it once and for all.

The boy, battling against the monster with all of his strength, made it to the edge of the woods and he could see the hut. There was no one else living near them to help; they had moved out of their little village to be on their own a while ago. And their families lived in villages further away. But it did not matter. The boy knew he just had to get to his sweetheart and, between them, all would be well. It always was and it always would be. He knew that for sure, with all of his heart.

Step by step, the boy crossed the plain, the monster thrashing and beating at him with its tentacles, as if it knew that the boy and his sweetheart were about to rise up and fight it to the death. Five, four, three, two steps, and one. The boy was at the opening of their hut. With a final furious struggle, he dragged himself in, ready to turn and fight his tormentor alongside his loved one.

The hut was empty, except for his own few possessions. His sweetheart had gone and had taken everything else. She had left him. Gone, for ever. The boy somehow managed to turn, the monster now still and watching him with its malevolent eye, and staggered out back on to the plain. He collapsed, sobbing, and lay there for what seemed an age. The monster waited, as if relishing the boy's heartbreak until, eventually, the boy twisted and turned on to his back and faced the monster rising up above him, ready to strike. 'Enough. Kill me, kill me now,' begged the boy.

The monster pulled itself up and its tentacles slowly started to writhe and thrash above the boy's head. The boy, defenceless, shut his eyes and waited for the monster's death blows. One second passed, and then another. One more and the boy opened his eyes to see the monster had stopped and turned to stare towards the woods. The boy followed the monster's malevolent glare.

The boy's father stood on the plain. He looked as though he'd rather be anywhere but here, but he was carrying a sharpened stick and took a slow and careful step towards the monster. Next to him, the boy saw his mother, a long-suffering expression on her face, appear brandishing a knife, and she started moving towards the monster too.

Then his sister stepped between the two of them. She didn't have a weapon but she had the loudest voice the boy had ever heard in his life and she could shout longer than anyone he'd ever met. Then his younger brother joined them. He looked confused, but at least he was facing the right direction. Finally, as the boy rose on to his elbows, he saw their dog come running out of the woods, joining the family as they advanced upon the monster...

Part Three

INSIDE THE
MAITLAND FAMILY

So, we come to Part Three of the book, with Michael really and truly at rock bottom this time – mentally ill, his marriage over and wanting to die. Niamh, having been with Michael for some eight years, ended their relationship and that was pretty much the end of him.

This third and final part takes us inside the Maitland family from May 2015 to the summer of 2017. We begin just a few days after the Ipswich v Norwich Championship Play-Off Semi-Final and that call from Niamh to Sophie asking for the phone to be passed to Tracey. Iain rushed in to shout, 'Is she pregnant!?' and then thought better of it.

May 2015

THE END OF MICHAEL

I knew from the look of utter desolation on Tracey's face as she listened to Niamh that Michael had died. I'd been with Tracey for 36 years at this point and I had never seen anything like that look ever before.

'Michael?'

She nodded but then added, 'They're breaking up.'

A surge of relief as I fought back tears. I thought we had lost him.

It was made worse somehow – much worse really – by the fact that I had thought all was well with them, that we'd all been watching football on the telly just a day or two before with everyone seeming happy. So ignorant was I of what was going on that I thought the call was to announce a pregnancy (as if such a momentous moment would warrant no more than a cursory phone call). I never expected this at all. I thought they would always be together. Michael and Niamh were a single being.

There was a toing and froing of texts between Tracey, Niamh and Michael, and then Tracey drove over to their home to bring Michael back.

Adam and I sat back down and continued watching an old DVD of *The Six Million Dollar Man* on the television, my mind racing and twisting and turning over everything. Halfway through the programme, I stood up and said that we'd better get the box room ready. Futon opened out, a sheet, a duvet added, a dust and a tidy round the room as best we could and an attempt by the three of us – Sophie, Adam and me – to make it look as homely as possible.

We waited for Tracey and Michael to arrive, which they did some 20–30 minutes later.

I stepped onto the driveway, Tracey climbing out of her car, Michael, slumped forward, staring into space, broken.

Tracey signalled at me to come forward, to help her get him out of the car.

On the edge of breaking down, struggling with my composure, I could not do it, but just stood there, watching.

Tracey gestured to me again, once, then twice.

Eventually, I moved, walking over, opening the boot, taking out his bits and pieces, doing a dad thing, being practical.

Tracey got him out of the car, and he stood there in front of me. An utter horror of a moment.

I patted him on the shoulder, unable to speak. Useless. The best I could do.

We all walked into the kitchen which is at the back of our house by the driveway. Sophie and Adam moved forward and the three children embraced. The sweetest touch.

Michael was home – but as I stood there looking at him, I thought this would be his last night on earth.

THOUGHTS ON SUICIDE

If a loved one is suicidal, there is plenty of advice out there, although, given that this is life or death, it's wise to take proper medical advice rather than digging deep into the sometimes murky world via Google. The NHS offers guidance, suggesting that if you are faced with someone having suicidal thoughts, you encourage them to talk about their feelings and listen to what they say without making judgements or trying to offer a solution. It's advice that is appropriate to any form or degree of mental illness really. The NHS uses the words 'reassurance', 'respect', 'support' – and that pretty much sums it up.

To encourage someone to open up, it's a good idea to use open-ended questions that make them talk and explain. So, you might say, 'What happened this morning?' and 'How do you feel about that?' The key is to get them to tell you what's in their mind and in their heart. You need to avoid closed questions where a 'yes' or 'no' or other end-of-conversation reply can be given. 'Did you see your boss today?' and 'Did you get the bus?' are two examples. You want to avoid the 'Yes, and I don't want to talk about it' response.

What you are trying to do here is to encourage them to tell their story, how they feel, what they're going to do, without leading them at all. As parents, for example, I think it's often, consciously or subconsciously, the case that you can see the solution – you may be screaming inside it's so obvious – and that you try to lead your child towards what you think is the right place to be. I've certainly tried to do this. It's wiser, I think, to let them come to their own conclusions, even if these are not what you want them to be.

It's best to avoid leading questions that, subtly or not so subtly, take them towards where you want them to go.

'This Chris doesn't sound a very nice person, does he?' would be one that the person asking the question has pretty much answered already. 'Have you thought about changing your job – how would you go about doing that?' is another. Not much point in asking these leading questions!

So, open questions get them talking. Closed questions shut them down. Leading questions take them where you, but not necessarily they, want to go. You can turn closed and leading questions into open questions with just a pause or two and a rephrasing. So, 'Do you have problems with your immediate supervisor?' isn't really getting you far, whereas rewording it to 'Tell me about your relationship with your immediate supervisor' opens everything up.

Although a conversation of this kind can provide some temporary respite, if someone is talking about taking their own life, this is something that really needs professional help as soon as possible. In much the same way that Michael's anorexia – truly awful though this is – was a consequence of his depression and anxiety and a need to have control over something, talk of suicide is, for want of a better expression, a symptom not a cause. Getting through this moment is one thing; addressing those underlying causes and managing them is another.

A GP is a good place to start getting help, for them and for their loved ones – never forget the loved ones who suffer too. More on that shortly, but for now let's get back to our story with the words of the NHS offering advice about suicide ringing in our ears: 'If there is an immediate danger, make sure they are not left on their own.' Yep, so guess what we did next...

THE NIGHT OF THE LONG KNIVES

I remember the three of us – Michael, Tracey and me – sitting in the lounge talking, some time later that evening after Michael had unpacked his belongings into our tiny, cramped box room.

I did not know at the time, but found out later, that, whilst we talked, Sophie took every knife and sharp implement out of the kitchen and hid them away. Adam emptied the cupboards of anything that Michael could swallow to take his own life.

Tracey tried to talk normally to Michael, to get him to think straight, to settle him, to try to set out what he was going to do: to keep going with his master's so he could get that in the summer and then find a job, to maybe see friends again, to come out with us, to do things, to keep busy.

I tried to listen to the conversation whilst texting Niamh at the same time, 'Will you give it another go?' (No.) 'Is it definitely over?' (Yes.) Niamh would help us, meet us, talk us through Michael's many issues, support us as best she could, but the marriage, her relationship with Michael, was over. She had to save herself. And who, frankly, could blame her?

I started scrolling through old emails, searching for contact details for the Priory. Could we get him back in that night? I wondered whether we should call the police, an ambulance maybe, try to get him into hospital, have him sectioned, whatever. We needed proper professional and medical help – and fast. This was way beyond our know-how. We had no idea what to do, were wholly unprepared for this unexpected and terrible turn of events.

I did not know how we would cope with any of this. By now, we were a family of four again at home, Sophie having completed her degree the previous summer and now on a teacher training course. Adam was literally in the middle of GCSE examinations. What could we do? What should we do? We did not know.

To me, Michael was on the brink of insanity that night. Adding grief and suicidal thoughts into his mix of mental ill-health – depression, anxiety, self-loathing and more – took him to the edge of the abyss.

Round and round we went, over and over, again and again. Would we talk to Niamh, make her see him, give him a chance to explain? No, we said, it's over. But if he could only see her one more time, maybe he could sort it out. Just one chance, please. There was never a chance. There was no point pretending there was.

Better still, he said, if we could get him a job via a contact in America, now, tonight – we had to promise – he could fly out there after completing his master's in the summer and start a new life. He'd he happy and accomplished, successful – all would be well. Where do you start? He hated his life here, but how could we let him go? I did not know whether to laugh or cry.

I looked at this stick-thin, broken boy, completely removed from all sense of reality, and wondered, not for the first time, how it had all come to this. I could not see how there was any way back for him this time. Or us.

Mental illness affects not just the sufferer but their family too. Adam had grown up from childhood – he was eight when Michael went away – with Michael's shadow over him. Most boys look up to a big brother; not so Adam. Now Michael was back, about to kill himself as Adam did his GCSE exams. And Sophie? They seemed so close as children; now she was hiding those long knives away. A nurse now, not a sister.

And Tracey and me? I had a terrible vision of Tracey, in her eighties, with me long dead, living here in this house, still with Michael in the box room, rocking to and fro, shuffling up to the Co-op in his slippers with a carrier bag, to buy vegetables, once a day. Then, when Tracey had gone, Michael – 'Creepy Uncle Michael' to his nephews and nieces – would end up in the spare room of Sophie's or Adam's house. When would this nightmare ever end for all of us? The day he died? Surely only his death would end this nightmare.

And so, as we went on and on, round and round, back and forth, we moved into the night and finally – tense, worried, exhausted by it all – we went to bed. Tracey and I to our bedroom up in the loft. Sophie to her bedroom on the middle floor, to the front of the house. Adam, to his bedroom on the middle floor, to the other side of the front of the house. And Michael, with a fresh month's supply of heavy-duty antidepressant tablets in his back pocket, to his little room on the middle floor at the back of the house.

AN URGENT RESPONSE TO SUICIDE

If you have someone with you, or close by you, who you think is going to commit suicide, the NHS advice is that if they have already been diagnosed with a mental health condition, you should contact their care team or wherever they have been treated. If you don't have these details, the NHS suggests you get in touch with the nearest accident and emergency department and ask for the details of the local crisis resolution team, the CRT.

This team comprises a range of mental healthcare professionals, psychiatrists and nurses, who are used to working with mentally ill people, and they will, in such an extreme situation, send someone out to you. I've spoken in more recent times to many people who have either had suicidal thoughts or who have had a loved one talking of suicide and I have been told regularly by them that once you get through (sometimes accessed via a GP), the response is usually swift and effective.

The NHS advice is that whilst you are waiting for them to arrive, you 'remove any possible means of suicide from the person's immediate environment such as medication, knives, household chemicals such as bleach and ropes or belts'. Stay with the person too, of course, and keep them talking. Keeping them away from alcohol and recreational drugs is a must as well; these could tip them over the edge.

Having talked to many people about mental health issues over the years, a surprisingly common approach at this unbearable time is to try to encourage the sufferer to agree to wait 24 hours before taking their own life. Negotiate, beg, plead – I don't know how you'd do it – but the idea seems to be that you'll agree to them taking their own life if they'll only promise they'll wait just 24 hours for you. In that time, you have the breathing space to get professional help.

We did not do any of this, although we desperately wanted to talk to someone – we were walking a tightrope here and felt that Michael would have reacted badly to suggestions that he gave us details of his care team so that we could contact them. It seemed to us that Michael thought he was talking rationally and sensibly – he was off the scale completely – and to imply otherwise might have been detrimental to him. We could have contacted the Priory but we were aware that Michael had been referred there by the NHS and to access them again would have meant having to follow that same route. That was a non-starter.

We did not make the call to the CRT – partly because at the time we did not know this system was in place or how to access it. Had we done something, we would have called 999 and asked for the police or an ambulance to take us to A and E and, explaining what the situation was, I would hope that somehow the nearest crisis resolution team would have been alerted and acted to help us.

Our view at this time – of GPs, the NHS and the help available – was that the support network for those with mental health issues was non-existent. Michael and Niamh had a while back talked of Michael's attempts to get help from one GP after another in Norfolk and Suffolk, and Michael felt they did little more than peddle pills. At one stage, I had spoken to a GP at my local practice about Michael and was so upset by their response – in essence, 'he's not our patient' – that I walked out of the meeting halfway through and immediately transferred to another practice.

If we had called the police or an ambulance – and we thought long and hard about it – we felt sure that, apart from ruining everything between us with a fatal loss of trust, they would drag Michael away kicking and screaming and have him sectioned, locked up, force-fed, in a straitjacket, never to be seen again. We could not bear that for him or that we had let him down in that way. I think these are mental images from our childhood, of how things were done in a less kind and more brutal age for mental health sufferers. But we are, to a certain degree, products of our upbringings and the views and thoughts from those long-gone days, and so we decided, at least for tonight, to see things through ourselves somehow.

A word on 'being sectioned' – that is, being taken to hospital and detained under the Mental Health Act. Someone can be detained if they have a mental illness that needs to be assessed and/or treated in hospital, is sufficiently serious that it endangers their health and safety and those of others around them, and they are unwilling to go in on a voluntary basis. (When Michael went to the Priory, he went in on a voluntary basis but would likely have been sectioned if he had not.)

Being sectioned usually begins when someone is worried about a person with mental ill-health; for example, a parent may call that person's GP or might phone for the police. The decision is normally made, except in an emergency, by two doctors and what's known as 'an approved mental health professional', an AMHP. One doctor must be certified as having experience of mental illness. Ideally, the other doctor will know the person. The AMHP may be a social worker or a mental health nurse, typically. The assessment lasts for up to 28 days. The treatment lasts for up to six months but can be renewed for another six months. No matter how agonising everything now was, we did not want that for Michael.

A SLEEPLESS NIGHT

Tracey and I lay in our bed in the loft, door ajar, now in the early hours of the morning, listening.

Tracey said, 'Sophie's taken all the knives, Adam's taken all the tablets.'

We lay there a while longer, reassured that Michael was safe, and we maybe started nodding off for a moment or two, exhausted.

I could not remember if I'd turned the key in the lock on the window in his room. If I had done, I could not recall pocketing the key. I mulled it over. No matter. The window didn't open very wide, not enough for him to climb out anyway.

He was safe in that room, for sure, just as long as he stayed there.

All I had to do was to lie here and listen to hear if he opened his door. If he did and went to the toilet, fine. I'd settle back down. If he went down the stairs, I'd have to get up, go after him, maybe stop him leaving the house, heading for the Orwell Bridge.

We'd then have to call 999, have him locked up, knowing we could never sleep if he was in the house, ready to kill himself at any moment. An awful, unthinkable thought. We could not bear it.

So we lay there a little longer, still believing Michael was safe, maybe drifting in and out of sleep again.

And then, with all the things that he could do in my mind, it occurred to me. 'Is he on medication at the moment?'

Long pause. 'He's just gone back on it, this last week, I think.'

So we lay there, fully awake now, each of us trying to work out whether taking a month's worth of antidepressants in one go could kill him.

Did he have water with him? Could he swallow 30 tablets one after the other without water? Yes, I guess so, if he was determined to kill himself. So, do I go down there and burst in? See him lying there, maybe awake and in tears?

Or asleep?

Or close to death, now needing to call an ambulance, have his stomach pumped?

How long, after he had taken all the pills, could he survive?

We lay there longer, not hearing any sound, no movement at all.

We had heard nothing since he went to bed.

Asleep?

Lying there?

As the clock turned 4am, I could stand it no more. Got up, decided to go to the toilet, knock on his door as I went by.

'You okay, Michael?'

Long, long silence.

A voice, finally. 'Yes.'

I went in.

He was alive.

THE ROUTE THROUGH TO
GET MENTAL HELP

Getting help for someone with urgent mental health issues, at the point where they might take their own life, is straightforward in principle if not in practice. You need to contact the local crisis resolution team, CRT, or whatever it is called locally. I suspect that many people, faced with such a gut-wrenching scenario, are as likely to call 999 or, if they can, take their loved one to A and E themselves, as they are to try to navigate their way through an unfamiliar system.

If you or a loved one is not at, or close to, the edge but is heading that way, you should know that, these days, there is a huge amount of help and support out there for you. That's not to say it is as simple and as direct a route as you might like, and some people have likened it to a maze at times.

You have to find your own way through. Different systems seem to be in place in different areas with different names. If I speak to a mental health expert in one part of the country, they will sometimes say one thing, using different terms and names compared with someone else at the other end of the country. City, rural – it's not as standardised as it could be.

There are official and self-help routes. Some of the people working in the system are more tuned in than others.

Don't be put off, though – it's all there for you. Here are some simple generic 'how-to' suggestions that should see you through one way or the other. The best place to start is your GP (or *a* GP, if you find your own GP is not as receptive as you would like). They can offer some short-term fixes – the medication that Michael so disliked but which works for many – and act as a signposting service for what's available locally such as self-help groups. They can explain the system where you are.

As an aside, you should find that there is someone in each GP practice with responsibility for mental health matters so, when making contact, you may want to ask if you can see that person rather than your usual GP (if they are not one and the same). You can, by the by, write a letter to your GP setting out what is happening – you can send this and they may then call you or you could take it with you to make sure you remember everything you want to say. Some people find this an easier, less daunting way to start the conversation than sitting in a room, trying to explain it all, step by step, to a GP you may not have seen for ages (or at all).

Also, your loved one may not yet be ready to seek help, but you can still go along and get advice on what's happening and some support too – and for you as well, because you need to look after yourself so that you can stay strong and help your loved one. Don't forget you, and other loved ones such as brothers and sisters. Note: The GP will not discuss specific cases or share medical records but they should talk in general terms about, say, what a parent might do if they had a child with, for example, depression.

One more aside, GP practices have limited budgets, so you may have to push to get referred up the line and you may have to go to a mental health charity or a private therapist to get long-term help with CBT and the like.

Your GP can direct you to the Community Mental Health Team (CMHT), or whatever it is called where you are. This comprises mental health experts – psychologists and community psychiatric nurses (CPNs), for example. In some areas you, or your loved one, may be able to self-refer to this service. Sometimes, the referral needs to go via a GP.

As an alternative, perhaps because your loved one does not want to see a GP, there are many voluntary organisations that can help. An informal service, run by volunteers who have often experienced the same issues, feels an easier way through for many. It was for us – the morning after Michael came home, we talked and, between us, Michael agreed to meet someone, a counsellor, to see if that would help. I trawled the internet, through all the main (good and worthy) charities – MIND, Samaritans, SANE, etc. – and found Suffolk User Forum, a 'mental health service user-led charity for Suffolk working to promote emotional and mental health for all'.

Suffolk User Forum offered to come out, talk to us, meet us individually and/or as a family; whatever they could do, they would. The woman we spoke to there – brilliant and lovely and wonderful and kind – had experienced depression herself to the point where she had called the local crisis resolution team at bad times and knew better than most what Michael was experiencing.

We also found, as you will do, that there are all sorts of local groups – where we are, for example, there are various eating disorder groups that can be attended by sufferers and/or their loved ones (there are separate sessions for parents and family to gain understanding and share worries). We did not progress this as we always felt that Michael's anorexia was, without wishing to downgrade this horrible illness, a knock-on effect of his depression and anxiety. Those issues – and the grief and the sense of possible suicide – were more pressing.

Suffolk User Forum – you may Google for similar services near you – also put us in touch with therapists who can offer a range of services; these, often after an initial free 30-minute, get-to-know-you session, are charged for – anywhere from £25 to £50 an hour and upwards. I believe that such services are available via the NHS if you meet key criteria but there are long waiting times. We could not wait and, having the money, went down the therapist route as soon as we could.

A word here about money. Much of the help that's available is provided by the NHS or free, or at low cost, via charities and self-help groups. But there are always issues of limited resources, especially in the NHS, and some services, such as counselling via therapists, do tend to have long waiting lists and limited availability.

Much will depend on how severe and urgent the mental health issues are. (All mental health issues are severe and urgent to the sufferer and their loved ones, but the NHS and other care providers will have their own criteria.) I believe, and I suspect it is sometimes a naïve belief, that the NHS comes through in times of great emergency; they almost certainly saved Michael's life by referring him to the Priory.

June 2015
Hitting rock bottom

It's been a while since I wrote anything and I don't really know what to write. I feel so broken, like I'm dead inside. I haven't stopped crying. I feel like I've lost everything and all I know. Imagine being with someone for eight years, going through so much, good times and bad times, and then suddenly they've gone. I've lost my wife, my home, my friends, and I feel alone. I feel I'm rock bottom.

When I came back, my brother went round the house hiding all the knives and pills because he saw I've lost hope. I really don't know what to do any more. I try to pull myself up each day but I don't really think I can keep going.

I've experienced a lot of pain in the past, but this is the most pain I've ever felt. I can't sleep, I just lie here crying and thinking about getting in my car and going.

I want to die.

* * *

How can I just get up and keep going? It feels impossible to me. I don't even know what to do with myself. I feel desperate. I'm now sitting here on my own and it feels like my world has fallen apart around me. My family are at work. I don't talk to my friends. I'm lost.

I've sat alone in my room now for days on end and it feels like the pain is getting worse. I feel heartbreak but I also feel physical pain. It's hard to describe how I feel. It's like my insides have been torn out. This is the worst pain I've ever felt.

My dad keeps trying to talk to me, but I can't listen to him. My head is full, but I also feel so empty. He wants me to see someone before it's too late, I think. I really don't feel up to it. I can barely leave my room.

* * *

My mum and dad made me go out with them for a drink. I look a mess. My hair is scruffy, I smell and my clothes are awful. I've struggled to do anything apart from cry. I have told my friend Adam and I can tell he's worried. He wants to see me. Probably to make sure I'm not going to do anything stupid.

I went for a drink with my mum and dad. We went to Costa, and as my parents were paying for drinks and I sat down at a table surrounded by people, I saw it was pretty busy. I just sat there empty, staring into space. My parents came over and we all sat there awkwardly.

I started crying in front of everyone. I kept saying sorry to my parents because I thought I was embarrassing them. You know someone's in a pretty bad way if you see them crying in public. My dad kept saying it's okay, don't worry about it. I was embarrassed but I felt too sad to stop.

THE DARKEST DAYS

One of the hardest things to handle when Michael came home was that he was understandably overwhelmed by grief and, we suspected, still suffering from various mental and physical issues; he wasn't as thin as he had been but he was nowhere near looking physically well. He also seemed to think he was sane and rational, but much of what he said – getting a job in the US, for example – suggested to us that he was anything but. We thought that, first and foremost, this was all caused and driven by grief. That needed to be addressed before anything else.

We made a conscious decision to talk to him as if he were perfectly fit and well mentally and physically; we felt that to suggest otherwise would have caused a major rift between us and knocked him down even further (if that were possible). So, yes, we could talk about America later in the year once he'd completed his master's. Meanwhile, we thought – as there was some resistance to any mention of GPs and the Priory – we would try to get him talking to a therapist once or twice a week who we hoped could steady him and set him back on the right track. And we would focus on being there as best we could through this initial grief too.

Where to start? Michael was a lost soul at this time and everything he had relied on – in essence, Niamh – was gone. (Niamh was gone for good, although she said she would always be there to help us – Tracey, Iain, Adam and Sophie – through. I did go and see her early on, mainly to collect the rest of Michael's things, and she was the same and as friendly as ever, and we talked for an hour or two about Michael and stuff, with me wobbling and catching my breath occasionally as it became clear there was no coming back for him.)

Michael did start to get up and get out and about during the days, buying vegetables and bits and pieces at the supermarket and cooking them. I tried to keep him busy with odd bits of research work for my writing. And he came with Tracey and me to garden centres and coffee shops and walks with Bernard the dog – anything to get him out of the house.

He went to the cinema with us and Sophie and Adam, and we all tried to nudge him along in our own ways. Most of the time he seemed dazed and tearful, and I'm not sure I was much use to him. My best advice – pretty much only advice – was along the lines of 'You just have to keep going, get through today as best you can.' What else was there to say at such a time?

It was hell, complete and utter. For Michael, of course – and for us too. The waiting each morning to hear a noise from his room, revealing he was still alive. The counting of the minutes as he went out, working out how long it would take to drive to the supermarket, go round it and come back. The constant looking at the clock when he had not returned. Texts – 'Can you pick me up this? Can you get that for me?' – to check all was well and to keep him going. The panic when we'd go out and, coming back, notice his car wasn't there. I felt as though I had a tight metal band round my head and felt physically sick all the time.

Listening each evening as he'd prepare his own evening meal. Vegan and, following Niamh's lead, now wanting a gluten-free diet, this usually comprised a huge pile of vegetables which he'd prepare for himself. He'd then disappear off to his room, Sophie and Adam checking on him now and then. Round and round. On and on. A never-ending story. And so the days passed, oh-so-slowly, and it seemed a long and endless time as Michael edged his way back from the dead.

DEALING WITH GRIEF

So, how did we help Michael with his grief? Overall, we just tried to 'be there', not too close, not too far away, and we let him fit back into the family as suited him. We tried to let him go at his own pace, to do things as and when he was ready. Dealing with someone who is experiencing grief is hard – it's difficult to know what to say and do. What we did, from reading around the subject, seemed to tick many of the 'must do' advice. More by luck than good judgement, I suspect.

We didn't talk of the past – too much pain there – and we didn't try to portray a really rosy future for him either. In effect, we stayed in the present, 'in the now', and just tried to help him through the day. To begin with, we looked no further than the film we'd see at the cinema the next weekend. We saw a lot of films with Michael, mostly obscure and foreign subtitled films that Tracey and I wanted to go to at the Ipswich Film Theatre. I can't imagine he really wanted to see them. But it got him up and out. Staying in the moment seems to be a good approach according to the experts. As time passed, we looked a little towards the future: a short break, a visit to a convention, seeing friends.

We let Michael work through his grief in his own way and time (albeit with professional help from a therapist). Grief is very personal and phrases such as 'I know how you feel', although meant well, are really not that helpful to the one who is experiencing grief. The person saying such a thing is almost taking over as if they are the person suffering. We all know people who say that and then proceed to share their own experiences as if these are somehow more important and relevant. They're not. Let the person grieving lead the way. Clichés such as 'Time is a great healer' and 'Plenty more fish in the sea' don't help either (although, in my own clumsy way, I think I did mention the time thing once or twice).

Stay truthful. Early on, Michael wanted us to contact Niamh to arrange a meeting, was going to go over and see her, was going to try to win her back. Having spoken to Niamh, that was never ever going to happen. We told Michael that when he raised the matter. Not easy for him, nor for anyone. But it's important, I think, for someone grieving to know what's what; some stuff can be fixed, some stuff can't. As we've mentioned before, earlier in the book, it's good to focus on what you can change and, however impossible it seems, to let the rest go.

'Go with the flow.' In many ways, if you are facing someone overcome with grief, it is hard to lay out the path through because you have to be led by them and their ever-changing emotions. It's often said that someone experiencing grief goes through various stages and you'll see four, five and seven stages listed in different books. Denial, anger, bargaining, depression were the key ones we saw in Michael, often ebbing and flowing, coming and going, changing places and coming back again, before he finally came to the final one, acceptance. That was, at this time, a long time off.

Seeing therapists

I'm still trying to write my gaming reviews but it's a real struggle. I can barely do anything. My main aim at the moment is to simply get through the day and not do anything stupid or cry or have a panic attack when I go round Tesco.

I try to distract myself. It sounds stupid but drawing and gaming is what helps me. I have been playing a game called *The Witcher 3*. It gives me a chance to escape real life and this hell for a short period of time – that and drinking rum. I've probably been drinking too much. I have explained to the guy I write reviews for about my situation and he's been very understanding. I want to do more, though, to try to take my mind off things.

My dad keeps looking around for therapists for me to see. It's frustrating me, though, because I'm only down because I have broken up with Niamh. I wasn't actually in that bad a place. This has made me be my worst. Niamh and I just didn't connect any more. We didn't speak. She would stay behind late at work. She was never there.

My dad has asked if I want to see a male therapist called Ray. My dad says he is an expert and his strength and positive mind power are so strong that he can fix anyone. I think my dad has been watching too many superhero movies. I said I'll go, just on the off chance it means I won't kill myself.

* * *

I just got back from seeing the therapist. I went in not really knowing what to expect. I feel broken and numb, although I thought I might as well see what he had to say. He seemed all right at first and we talked around stuff about me and that was okay. But then he asked me how I was feeling at that moment. I said I felt like crap.

'No, you don't.'

'Er, yes I do.'

'No! You don't.'

'Um, I do actually.'

'NO YOU DON'T!'

It went on and on like this until I said, 'Well, I thought I was going to kill myself.' He then changed the subject.

I didn't really click with him, lol.

* * *

I'm home and alone in my room again. I hate that I feel stuck. Where do you turn when you have lost everything? What do you do? How do you start? I wish that I could just move away, go somewhere else and begin again. Meet new people and start a different life. I'm sick of always feeling pain. I can't see how this is going to feel better.

* * *

I want to buy a bike and start going for bike rides. I've done nothing in ages.

* * *

My mum and dad thought a bike was a good idea so I've just got back from buying a new bike. It's a road bike, which I've never used before. I think I'm going to start planning some routes and going for rides.

* * *

I've just spoken to my dad and he says he has found another therapist for me – great. I can't even count how many different people I have had to talk to over the years, with no positive outcome at all. I now find it hard to think that it's going to work, especially when I'm feeling like this.

I'm going to see a woman called Suzanne who has suffered with issues herself in the past. At least I'm going to talk to someone who actually knows and understands what it's like. Most people who talk to you have no idea; they've just read a lot of books and think that makes them an expert. Most of them know nothing. It's embarrassing talking to someone who is trying to help you when you know more than them. I always feel I have to help them to understand.

* * *

I just got back from seeing Suzanne, who is a hypnotherapist. I haven't tried this before, which is rare because I have pretty much tried everything you can think of at this point. My dad seemed excited about it and said he was interested to see who I'd come back as each week – Buzz Lightyear, the Incredible Hulk. I think my dad thinks hypnotherapy is the same as hypnosis. He said he'd seen a stage show of it once and I shouldn't dance round with a broom or drop my trousers. He means well.

I arrived at the clinic and walked in looking really rough: scruffy clothes, hair a mess and generally looking homeless. I had been crying that morning so I wasn't feeling at my best. I walked in and met her and I could tell she was a nice person, very smiley and kind. I could see from the look on her

OUT OF THE MADHOUSE

face, though, that she knew I was in trouble; she looked concerned.

I sat down in a chair and the session started with her asking me questions about my life and why I've got to this point. She asked me everything. About my family, upbringing, friends, work, school and all the in-between things. The main topic was obviously Niamh and what had happened. I explained how I feel sad, heartbroken, but I also feel a lot of anger. I can't really believe what happened.

After we talked for a while, we then came to the next part of the session which is the hypnotherapy. I reclined the chair and Suzanne put on smoothing music. It's hard to describe what happened next, but she talked the whole time with me dipping in and out of consciousness.

I always felt in the room. It's almost like being in that moment just before you fall to sleep. You're sort of there but you're not completely there. I remember her putting across positive thoughts and ideas.

The next part hit me hard. She said imagine you're on a beach. I thought of Antigua (where I married Niamh). Suzanne was describing my surroundings and said, 'Watch the waves slowly crash on the white sand.'

She then said, 'Draw a circle with your finger in the sand. Place all the sad things in your life or things that have caused you pain in that circle.' I put Niamh in the circle.

Suzanne then said, 'Take a moment to think about that. Then the waves roll in and wash away the circle and everything in it. They roll back in again and wash the remains away.' I felt tears roll down my cheeks. Niamh was gone.

I'm home now and thinking about the session. It hit me hard actually, but I think that I might give it another go and see what happens from there. My family are talking about going away on holiday soon and it would be good to have someone to talk to, apart from Bernard who sits there staring at me. I think he thinks I'm weird.

HOW TO COPE WITH PANIC ATTACKS

Michael has experienced panic attacks in the past and has recently expressed the fear that he might have another one at some point in a busy supermarket. A panic attack is sudden and can feel very violent; it's a mix of strong and overwhelming anxiety along with a potentially wide range of physical symptoms – most often, shaking, sweating, feeling breathless, going dizzy, a thumping heart.

Panic attacks have been likened to having a heart attack in their physical intensity and they typically last for between five and 20 minutes. It's as if you have lost control of your body. They are scary, both for those experiencing them and those who are watching; you will recall Michael's diary from the Priory when he wrote of a fellow patient who experienced such attacks in public. There are things to do, though.

Go with it

Panic attacks are driven by anxiety and it's important to remember this and that, despite how intense they feel, they do pass without causing damage. Many experts suggest you try to work through the attack if you can, rather than give in to it; if possible, try to carry on with what you are doing. By working through it, you'll realise – and it may take some time and many attempts – that what's happening is not as bad as it feels. Easier said than done, of course, at least to start with. It can help if you have someone with you who understands what's happening and can talk you through.

Breathe deeply

Michael found it helpful to close his eyes, focus on his breathing and count in and out up to ten, to calm himself at these times. You may do too, especially if you find your breathing is jagged and shallow. You should try to breathe in deeply and fully through your nose and then, at the same pace, breathe out through your mouth. Keep repeating this breathing exercise as you become calmer.

Learn to relax

Panic attacks are the body's 'fight or flight' reaction to something that causes extreme stress and anxiety. So, as part of your response, it's important to try to relax your body. One of the exercises we talked about earlier in the book, where you close your eyes and focus on relaxing each part of your body in turn, is effective for many people. You can start from your toes and work upwards, finally reaching your head and stilling your mind.

Think positively

When you are experiencing an attack, you need to try to remind yourself of several key points. 'It's "just" anxiety' (your body is not having a heart attack). 'Anxiety will pass' (just as it always does). 'I am in control.' Some people have said that they have benefited from chanting a mantra at these times: 'It will pass…it will pass' or 'I'm in control…I'm in control.'

Think ahead

You may want to take some preventative steps to avoid panic attacks, happening in the future or to reduce their severity, as far as you can anyway. Michael worked out in advance those trigger points that caused issues for him and tried to avoid them. So, for example, if you find that going into a supermarket at a busy and crowded time is likely to trigger an attack, you may want to go at quieter times whenever possible. That's an easy one for most people to spot; others may take time to identify. It can be useful to keep a diary of what happened and when.

Other ideas

Other advice from those who have experienced panic attacks and have worked through them involves routine, exercise, breathing and talking to fellow sufferers. Regular meals – good food and drink – can help steady blood sugar levels. Exercise – walking, stretching, running – is a plus. Doing breathing exercises regularly each day will make it easier to slip into these as and when you need to. Talking to others who experience these attacks, via your GP or an organisation such as No Panic (National Organisation for Panic, Anxiety Neuroses, Information and Care) will help as well.

July 2015
Seeing friends again

My friend Adam has texted me because he wants to see me. He has been trying to contact me because I think he knows how bad I can get. I haven't seen him in a long time. I've known Adam since I was about five or six years old. We are going to go to the cinema to watch a film. He says try to do it because I need some sort of distraction.

* * *

I'm home again now in my room alone. I feel so lost. I don't even know what to do with myself. I have no proper job, find it hard to see people and all my belongings are in cardboard boxes on the floor.

I sleep on a futon and struggle to get up in the morning. I don't like going out because I see happy people, families and couples. I have always felt like an outsider for so long. I don't feel like a normal person. I know I'm weird.

We went and saw *Southpaw* and my brother came along too. It was hard to watch because it's a about a guy who becomes a famous boxer. At the start of the film he loses his wife and doesn't get to see his child any more. He starts drinking and loses everything. He has to start again from rock bottom. The film resonated a lot with me and it hit me pretty hard.

* * *

I find it hard to get up in the mornings and keep going. I don't like how I look or feel. I've been out in my car now and again, but as soon as I'm on my own, bad thoughts fill my head. Every day is a struggle and I feel nothing but sadness and pain.

Every time I drive over the Orwell Bridge, I think how easy it would be to stop the pain once and for all. I've tried for so many years to be happy. I've been sad for about the last eight years. Why would anyone keep going?

TIME TO TALK BODY IMAGE

Michael still had body image issues mixed in with grief and other mental health issues. Talking body image, Michael is six foot tall and, contrary to what he thinks, is nice-looking. (I'm his father, so I am biased, of course.)

When he was younger, he always seemed to be attractive to girls. If he went to Sophie's school to collect her in his car, all her friends would rush forward to look at him (much to Sophie's embarrassment). He never realised this and has always had issues with how he looks. It's not unusual with mental illness. Whether it's chicken or egg, I don't know – but it seems to feature as part of many issues. It's another tentacle.

I've spoken at lots of mental health events and, let's be frank here, some very attractive men and women have stood up to speak about their issues with body image and in my head I'm thinking, 'Seriously? Come on!' But they do have or have had serious problems. Internally, there are mental health issues. Externally, there are pressures from peer groups, advertising, social media and more, all suggesting what the perfect look is. Coming to terms with how you look isn't easy, but you should hopefully be working towards these goals.

Be grateful

Whatever's in your head, something's right about your body. It's breathing, it's moving. All being well, it allows you to read, listen to music, go for a walk, drink a long cool glass of water, eat a hot meal. That's a lot of pluses. It's not easy to feel grateful for what you've got – human nature always wants more – but it's something to aim for.

Years ago, I broke my left ankle. I had to go in and out of hospital over a few months. One day, on crutches, I had to get the bus home. I huffed and puffed my way to the bus stop, waited there for ages, struggled theatrically on to the bus, and sat down heavily, moaning to the person nearest to me about how awful it was being on crutches. The guy had a club foot.

Stay positive

Your brain sends out messages, both positive and negative ones. If it's sending out negative ones, by and large, everything you think is downbeat; you feel stressed and anxious, you see every spot, line or grey hair (depending on your age), and everything's generally just dreary and miserable. You don't like your hair, your face, your nose, the shape of your body, the length of your legs – on and on it goes.

You can help your brain to send out good messages by looking after your body, getting plenty of sleep, eating healthily and drinking well so you stay hydrated, taking exercise, relaxing and meditating regularly. You can also work on turning these negatives around. When you are conscious that your brain is 'saying' something negative, you can state a positive, maybe repeating it as a mantra for a while.

Michael struggled for ages with his looks but always felt better when he thought about getting a haircut. So, his negative comment would be 'My hair looks awful' and his positive would be 'I'll look better once my hair's been cut today.'

Treat yourself as you do others

Many people with mental ill-health beat themselves up. Michael is a classic example. They feel depressed and anxious. They look in the mirror. Because they are down, they don't like what they see. Round and round it goes: feeling more depressed and anxious, feeling worse about their appearance and so on. You need to try to break the cycle.

When someone feels better – as Michael did in the hours after a haircut – thoughts about themselves tend to lift slightly. This is a good time to write down what you do like about your appearance, to be looked at during the next dip. Some sufferers, when they feel negative about how they look, say (out loud when possible), 'That's not true!' It's important to work on being kind to yourself rather than putting yourself down. Think about this approach – if you'd not say that to a friend, don't say it to yourself.

Other thoughts to consider

'Body image' is, for many, wrapped up inside self-esteem issues. There are lots of things to consider that might help you, according to those who have experienced these. One is to remember that no one is 'perfect' (and what one person considers perfect won't be the same as someone else). Think of all the people you admire in one way or the other. The reality is that they probably don't look perfect and they won't have perfect lives either. They still get up in the mornings with drool on the pillow, have to use the bathroom, do all the same things anyone else has to do, talk to people, meet people, and find their way through to happiness.

Learn to accept compliments. If you feel down and someone says something nice to you – 'I like your hair' – it's instinctive to think 'Yeah, right' or 'Whatever.' You knock it back, dismiss it. It's better to try to suck it in and hold on to it – you could even have a little note of compliments you've received to check over at bad times. Give compliments too – you may then get more back. When you are receptive to these, they will lift you.

Recognise what you can change and what you can't. I have a huge head and a fat face – I'm fine with both although small children scream – and there's nothing I can do about them. I don't wear hats or sunglasses as they look silly on me and I don't have a short haircut which would draw attention to both. That's how I handle these things that, when I was younger, troubled me quite a lot.

By the way, if you don't like your size, shape or weight, please, please – *please* – don't diet. Just don't if you are vulnerable to mental health issues; it's a slippery slope. Focus instead on sleeping, eating, exercising and relaxing well and weight issues should become less significant.

August 2015
Summertime blues

I just got back from another bike ride. I have been enjoying going out on my bike and the freedom I feel it gives me. This time wasn't so good, though. A car clipped my back wheel and I came off my bike pretty badly.

My body hurts, especially my bum. I have been to the doctors and they have said I've cracked my bum bone, not sure how to spell it (coccyx). I feel in so much pain and find it hard to sit down. I'm now going to have to walk round like I've had some sort of toilet accident.

I haven't said anything to my dad about it as he'll start making terrible jokes. He may not notice anyway. Most of the time he's in a world of his own. My sister did something like this before (and probably screamed the house down). My dad bought her this weird cushion shaped like a ring doughnut. It's probably the most awkward cushion ever to sit on but it helps a bit.

* * *

I have been very low the last couple of days. My family spent ages deciding if they should go on their summer holiday this year and thought they would as it would be good to see how I manage on my own with Bernard. But now they are having second thoughts and keep saying they will just stay at home.

I want them to go, though. I need some time on my own to think. I will see Suzanne and see what she says when I see her in a couple of days. I'm off to university today (the course runs through into August). I've fallen a bit behind with work because my head has been all over the place recently and it's been hard to focus.

I've come so far, but at the same time I could so easily drop out. We have a big presentation coming up and a final master's exhibition which I need to get the work done for and then set up my space at the show. I've been going in to see Lee, one of my tutors, and he has been teaching me some cool animation techniques. I have also chatted to him about everything that happened to me, as he has been through a divorce in the past. It helps to talk to someone who's been there.

* * *

My family are on holiday and I have just got back home from seeing Suzanne. I'm seeing her for an extra session a week for the two weeks they are away. The session went well but it's also a weird feeling coming out of there. Sometimes I feel sad, sometimes I feel more relaxed and sometimes I feel confused.

What it does do, though, is make me think a lot about what has happened. She keeps telling me to focus on positives, but it's hard to find any when I've lost everything. I don't really know where I'm heading in life any more. We had it all planned out, with our house, cars and the possibility of children. I now sleep on a futon in a tiny bedroom, lol.

* * *

I have set up everything now for my exhibition. I had to sort out a big TV to play my animations on and have had a book printed up showcasing my illustrations. The show is in a couple of days and I will be going up by myself in the evening. My parents will see it when they get back from Spain.

I've been watching a lot of video game podcasts as gaming has always been one of my favourite things and an escape for me. I'm also trying to do more illustration and gaming reviews, just to keep myself going.

* * *

So I just went to my end-of-year show. I drove up to Norwich by myself. I got there a bit early so I went and sat in a café and had a coffee. That's when I started feeling sad because Niamh and I spent a lot of time together here in Norwich and I'm now sitting here alone. I watch couples and families walk by and it hurts me. I start to think, am I alone because I'm a really horrible person?

The show was a big event and I hung about looking scruffy, with my hoodie on and beanie. Everyone seemed to be dressed smart but me. I hadn't even thought about what I should wear.

We were meant to 'mingle' with people looking at our work. One man came up to me and asked me if I was on drugs when I did my work, which I think was a joke, so I just said I'm a bit mental. It was quite nice, though, seeing some people enjoying my work and saying nice things.

I didn't hang around too long and left to go home and get back to my bed and be alone. I'm feeling a little bit lost now because my master's has been my main focus for such a long time. I'm not sure what to do next.

MY ANIMATION WAS INSPIRED BY THE LEGEND OF ICARUS, WHO FLEW TOO CLOSE TO THE SUN.

CATCHING UP AGAIN WITH THE MAITLAND FAMILY

Michael aside for one moment, 2015 was a significant year for the Maitlands. Since 2011, when Sophie had left for university, the family at home had been Iain, Tracey, Adam and Bernard the dog. That all changed in 2015.

Sophie had come back from Durham University in the summer of 2014 and moved into her old room. She worked part-time, as she done through holidays for the past few years, at Cineworld in Ipswich. From September 2014, she gave that up to train as a primary school teacher.

In early 2015, she broke up with her boyfriend, Paul, after three or four years, met a new boyfriend, Glyn, in the middle of 2015 and, as we move towards the autumn of 2015, had won a 'best trainee teacher of the year' award for East Anglia and started a job at the local primary school, teaching five-year-olds.

Adam had done well enough in his GCSEs to go on to do A Levels at a sixth form college in Ipswich – English, Film Studies and Media Studies. He was not sure what he would do after that. He had a girlfriend, also called Sophie (a.k.a. 'Normal Sophie') and life was good for him.

Tracey was still working as a teaching assistant at the local primary school. She had now been doing this for more than eight years and thought that, at some point soon, she might do something different. She was not sure what that might be.

Having had my fill of writing about roof tiles and cow pats and sterling and forward contracts, I decided to become a creative writer from then on. In November, I had breakfast with a literary agent, Clare, who pitched my idea for a book of letters, *Dear Michael, Love Dad*, to a publisher at Hodder the next morning. Four hours later, I became a full-time creative writer.

So, as 2015 came to a close, the original family – Iain, Tracey, Michael, Sophie and Adam – was together again under the same roof, with Bernard the dog, of course. Michael, back in a warm and loving environment, showed signs of becoming well as the year passed – getting into a routine, doing some work, getting out and about, moving on from grief and seeming to handle his mental health issues. It was a slow and gradual process over months. So slow that no one really noticed. It looked as though 2016 would be a good year, though – maybe even a transformative one.

February 2016
My day-to-day life now

Life is much the same as usual. I get up slowly, shower, do my hair and have some breakfast, and then try to do a bit of work. I have started looking for jobs and have even been applying to video game companies. I spoke to a well-known guy from IGN and he did say he admired my persistence, but there's nothing available right now. He gave me some advice on my reviews. He told me how to structure them properly – put them into sections and then wrap it up at the end.

* * *

I've just got back from seeing Suzanne again, which went well. I still struggle day to day and sometimes I feel myself slipping again. I get like this when there's no one about and I start to feel very alone. I've spent so much of the last five years on my own. Hiding away from everyone, not wanting to speak or see people. I want to start seeing my friends Toby and Adam more, but I want it to be like it used to be. I'm not sure it can be really.

* * *

I've been to Norwich today and had a coffee with a guy called Peter. He saw my work at the university show last summer and said he was interested in working with me on some sort of stage show. When I met him at the end of last year, I could tell he was a kind man and he spoke very well. He had a fedora, which my dad would have liked. I was probably what he expected – a weird-looking art student/homeless person. That's the vibe I give off, with a bit of emo thrown in.

I sat and spoke with him for an hour or so and he told me about his ideas for the theatre production. He wants to adapt the James Joyce book *Ulysses* into a performance and is interested in me doing the design, backdrops and possibly animation segments.

I picked up *Ulysses* and have been attempting to read it. My dad said it was a pretty complex book like *War and Peace*; it wasn't a comic I could read in an evening. I still haven't finished it. I've seen Peter once or twice for updates. I don't think it's likely to happen but he's a nice man and it's worth a try. As my dad says, you never know.

I really don't know what to do in terms of work. I'm kind of holding on to this thing with Peter as at least it's some kind of project and might get my name out there. Although it seems a bit sad that my only hope is this. I would love to do something in the gaming industry and I think I know quite a lot about it. I also have good skills with writing reviews and making videos. I will keep pushing that and see if I can get anywhere with it. I have also applied for all sorts of other jobs. I do a bit of work for my dad and am going to do some illustrations for his books.

* * *

Getting divorced has to be one of the most depressing things ever. It's horrible. I get letters through the post sent from Niamh with bits I have to fill out, with copies of our marriage certificate. It also has written explanations from Niamh saying she wants a divorce. She said things like I neglected her, treated her wrong and she no longer loved me. I was in a bad place, though, and my mind was gone. I didn't care.

I look back now and we both were good at times but we were also bad. I think we were bad for each other. Towards the end it was pretty volatile and toxic. We didn't like spending time with each other. I didn't like spending time with anyone. I think I just hated everyone and everything. I need to move on from this and just try not to dwell on it.

LOVED ONES! LOOK AFTER YOURSELVES TOO

The focus of much of this book has been on Michael and those with mental ill-health rather than on us, the Maitland family, and the loved ones of others with mental health issues. Yet it is often family and loved ones who bear at least some of the brunt of what's happening. Niamh, who by this time was long gone from our lives other than an occasional 'Hi, how are you doing?' email from me, loved and supported Michael for so many years under what must have been unbearable pressure. We had a sense of what she had to live with when Michael came home to us, although, by now, the pressure was easing and we could see the way ahead. So, what should loved ones do for themselves?

Accept you're not to blame

For a long time after Michael went into the Priory, I blamed myself. How did I not see what was happening? Was our relationship so poor that he could not confide in me? Was there nothing I could have done to have saved him? These were the first three of a long list of reproachful and regretful questions that went on and on.

These three questions, or very similar, are fairly common ones asked by parents in these situations. I did not see what was happening for so long because it never occurred to me that something so awful could happen to such a happy family. Michael did not realise for a long time either. He then did not wish us to know, wanted to shield us from it. Michael did not confide in any of us – Tracey, Sophie, Adam or me – for the same reason. It's hard to save someone when you (and they) don't really know what's going on. Where do you start?

'These things happen' sounds trite but it's essentially true. We've likened it since, in talks, to something in Michael's brain simply clicking the wrong way, and that, rather than anything else, caused the depression and anxiety and everything that then happened. It's a nonsense, of course – there's no switch in Michael's brain mush, but it's as good a reason as any when there's nothing else obvious there to explain it. 'It's in the genes' is another expression we've used, although, in our case, there is no record of depression or mental ill-health in the immediate family.

Maintain your own health

You need to pay as much attention to yourself as you do to the one who is suffering from mental ill-health. Much of the how-to advice for them on looking after themselves is equally applicable to you. Sleep – enough of it, with a regular bedtime and a regular getting-up time – is important so that you can manage what takes place in between.

Eating well, at regular intervals – rather than snatching at snacks as and when you get a free moment – is essential too. As is exercise of some kind, even if it's a morning and evening walk with the dog, when you can take some time out, and maybe a walk around the block at lunchtime at work.

Those relaxation exercises from Part One of the book – breathing, perhaps breathing in time with your walking strides, and candle and visualisation techniques – once learned, can be helpful. You can use these to relax during stressful moments and flashpoints through the day.

Set some boundaries

When Michael came home that terrible night and I went in so early the next morning, we had a long and frank talk. Right or wrong, I said we would do all we possibly could to help him get better, but that if he was going down the pan, he'd be going down on his own. The rest of the family weren't going down and were not going to have their lives destroyed. I think it's called tough love.

I don't know if that was a good or bad thing to say; I suspect the latter. Even so, many experts, advising loved ones to look after themselves in such scenarios, do talk of setting boundaries as to what they will and won't do, and to speak up for themselves, telling the person with mental ill-health how you feel and if they are upsetting you.

This is something of a minefield and needs to be navigated carefully on a case-by-case basis. In terms of boundaries, we did make it clear that, for all that we would do, we were not – and, more specifically, Tracey was not – going to be his carer in the way that Niamh had become. He had to do things for himself, get up, get himself sorted, take care of himself, see a therapist, etc.

In terms of telling him how we felt, we did, at least in the early days, tread on eggshells around him. How do you begin talking about such an utter horror of a situation – that what was happening was killing us too? I am not sure if keeping quiet and screaming silently was a good or a bad thing to do. Again, I suspect it was the latter, but we were, for a good while, thinking he might take his own life. How would we live with ourselves if we contributed to that? As Michael started to improve and he returned to better health, we did start to speak up more. It's a matter of judging the moment.

Be organised

On a practical level, you need to be organised – dealing with someone with mental health issues is time-consuming; you are either doing something to help them or you are thinking and worrying about them. It cuts into your time.

A daily planner, a schedule and 'to-do' lists can all be helpful, as can setting aside specific times for yourself, whether that's to go for a walk or a run or to listen to music.

Some people in these situations even set aside 'worry times', when they will think about what's happening, on the basis that they can compact all their worries into those times only. It works for some.

Talk to someone about how you feel

This is key. Tracey and I would often talk about Michael and find ourselves playing 'good cop, bad cop' in that one of us would be angry about Michael in some way and the other would take a calmer, opposite view, seeing things from his point of view. Next time, our roles would somehow reverse – odd though this might be, it seemed to help us work things through in our heads to reach a balanced agreement.

Tracey would also talk to friends, at work and those she knew from out of work. Being a writer, sitting at a desk in the loft for 30 years, means I don't really have any close friends to talk to – and men, sigh, usually want to talk more about cars and crankshafts and other manly things that I don't properly understand.

It's important to talk to someone; a close friend or family member is often suggested. That may work for you, but you may prefer to talk to a professional who is independent and experienced in these matters. Too often, friends and family have some sort of emotional attachment and bias, and, just as likely, know someone who knew someone years ago who had someone who did something a bit like this (but much, much worse) and so they urge you to do this, that and the other. Friends and family may be well-meaning but often want to have their own input into something they don't really understand.

Your GP should be able to point you in the right direction of what's available locally in terms of counselling and local support groups and self-help organisations. For example, Beat, the UK charity supporting those affected by eating disorders, anorexia and other, food-, weight- and shape-related difficulties, has support groups for loved ones. They also have online chat rooms where fathers and mothers and loved ones can seek help (i.e. there are separate chat rooms for each). Increasingly, more and more charities have online and offline support networks in place. Go Google.

April 2016
Me and my tattoos

Today, I'm going to see Adam and Toby for a bit and I think we will probably go to the cinema. I also got an interview at a call centre so I will be going to that tomorrow.

* * *

I just went for an interview at a call centre in Ipswich. It was also a training day. I left pretty quickly without getting the job because it was the most depressing workplace I have ever seen. People moaning and sitting on phones. No one was smiling and, to be honest, I would have rather have killed myself than work there. I hadn't told anyone about the interview because it was just a shot in the dark. It's not what I want to do. I could not face that every day.

* * *

I've been seeing Suzanne for a while now and I'm slowly seeing her less and less. It started off at once a week or twice when my mum and dad were on holiday. I've been seeing her every other week. I can't say that I'm better, but I don't want to kill myself any more. I guess that's some sort of progress. Maybe that's my biggest achievement, not taking my own life. Not that big an achievement really. Unless you've been there, of course. Then it's huge.

* * *

I think I'm going to book another tattoo. I was thinking of getting a lighthouse with tentacles wrapping up around it. A lighthouse represents hope – light in the dark. And my favourite game has a big twist which features a lighthouse.

Lighthouses also appear in my drawings a lot in the distance. The tentacles represent how I feel about mental health.

I've always loved tattoos. I like that it's a different kind of art. I also seem to get tattoos done in times when things have been bad for me. My granny died a few years ago when I was at my worst and I could not face going to the funeral. My dad was really upset and angry about it. Afterwards, I had a tattoo done as a way of remembering her. I have always seen tattoos as a positive thing, although my parents may think otherwise. I don't think they like them very much.

I've got lots of tattoos on my chest and arms. I have a heart with wings on my chest. I had a forearm done but have now had that covered up because it was to do with Niamh (I put a big black skull over it). One sleeve has the word family with flowers around it. I got a rose done on that for my granny. Other roses and lilies are fillers on that sleeve. I am going to have a lighthouse on that sleeve too. My other sleeve has a clock with two turtle doves – love.

* * *

I am thinking of going to London Comic Con again later this year. My mum and dad got me a ticket last year and I went down and stayed overnight and had a look around. I'd always wanted to go.

As I got to the train station, I remember I almost didn't go because inside the whole time I was thinking how pathetic it was that I was having to do it on my own. A normal person would go with friends.

The convention was awesome, though, and I loved looking around. I got a couple of geeky figurines. I am actually a bit of a nerd when it comes to stuff like that. It was good to get out and do it, but at the same time it kind of highlighted that I'm a bit of a loner.

At least, though, I was able to pick myself up and go and do something. I think that it probably helped me in more ways than I even know. If I go again this year, I might try to go with my brother.

* * *

My dad's book is out soon and I have done a drawing of the two of us for the last page. I am looking out, smiling, with a thumb up and my dad has his arm round me. I quite like it. My dad says it is a poignant ending for the book.

TURN THAT 'VICTIM' MENTALITY AROUND

Although Michael is starting to sound upbeat now, there have been moments over the years (and in 2016 too) when I have felt that he believes, no matter what happens, he is always the victim. A sort of 'bad things always happen to me, no matter what'. I don't doubt there are times when he has been the victim, but having 'a victim mentality' is not helpful to good mental health. Experts offer lots of advice on turning this around and there are some common themes in what they say.

Identify the mentality

First things first, *you* – you being the person with a victim mentality – need to identify that there is a problem. In the short term, there can be a peculiar sense of pleasure in feeling hard done by – 'Isn't everyone awful to poor old me?' – and, at least to begin with, it can elicit sympathy from family and friends.

However, a victim mentality becomes very draining over time for everyone. It's hard to have good mental health if you always feel a victim. You're stuck in an endless loop of negativity.

It's worth trying to step back and look at something that has gone wrong recently. If you can see that you 'enjoy' telling people of the latest thing that's gone wrong in your life and/or you don't feel you can do anything about it, then there is an issue – and you've just identified it. That's the first step.

Take responsibility

You as a person are responsible for what happens in your life – your 'job', if you like, is to make things happen rather than let them happen to you. You may find it useful to make a list of areas where you feel hard done by, to see what you could have done, and could do for the future, to change the outcome.

Okay, it's not always possible. You've lost hours at work because of cutbacks. There's probably not much you can do about that, but how you respond – getting organised, applying for other part-time jobs, getting out and about and meeting people – is down to you. Maybe you cannot change what happened before, but you can change what happens next.

Learn forgiveness

Those with a victim mentality tend to be trapped in a culture of blame. To start with, they feel it's their fault that something went wrong. 'It always goes wrong for me, no matter what.'

Breaking free from self-blame, the next thought is often 'I'm not responsible, so someone else is to blame!' We live in a society where, whenever something goes wrong, someone always has to be at fault.

It's important to try to move on, to forgive and forget. Some people aren't nice and are out for themselves. Bad stuff happens to good people. It's life. You have to move forward from it.

Show gratitude

Remember those lists we talked about in Part One? The good things in your life? Lists like that play a key role in breaking free from this victim mentality.

When you have had a knock-back, you need to look at all the good things you still have in your life. Write them down, as you did before, with an upbeat friend and, if it helps you, carry the list around with you to look at during the day.

It's worth asking what you can draw from the experience that would normally have you feeling like the victim. Could you have been more active than passive when it happened? Might that have made a difference? What would you do to avoid it happening again? If it does happen again, what would you do?

May 2016
What my therapist does to help me

Seeing Suzanne seems to be helping me, but I'm not sure if it's because of the techniques she is using or the fact that I have someone I can talk to on a regular basis. Having someone to talk to is really important to me. I can talk about general stuff with my family and my friends, but it's good to have someone I can work through the crap with. I don't really want to talk to my mum or dad about stuff like that as they'd not really understand or know what to say. My dad would feel awkward and make a joke about something anyway. The sessions with Suzanne are good, though.

They always start the same. We talk for about 20 minutes and she asks me questions about how I've been getting on. Sometimes I've been fine and other times things haven't been so good. I'll talk these things through with her.

She tries to get me to focus on the good things and always suggests seeing friends more and trying to get out to do things. She then puts on calming music, which is about trying to get me to relax. I have gone in a few times really not feeling good and on edge, but she always helps me to chill out about whatever's bothering me. Music's helpful, I think.

Once the music plays, I then lie back and she says close your eyes. She talks slowly. I can't quite remember what she talks about but I know that what she says, although I may not remember it, is actually being taken in by my subconscious. It must work in some sort of way because I do leave feeling a lot better.

Coming round is the weirdest part. At the end of being under, Suzanne counts down slowly from ten to one and every time I seem to come back into the room when she gets to about three. I don't even know why my body suddenly wakes up again but it always happens.

Suzanne has also given me a CD to listen to at home when I feel stressed out – it's just relaxing music and I put it on when I am trying to meditate. I do it when I feel sad or when I'm angry. My sadness generally has turned into anger. I'm not normally an angry person – I'm usually chilled out – but the more I think about things that have happened, the more I get frustrated. I think maybe anger is better than feeling sad. Sadness makes me feel I've given up. Anger makes me feel I am fighting back.

UNCOMFORTABLE TRUTHS ABOUT MENTAL ILL-HEALTH

We've learned many things about mental health on Michael's journey and, as we come into some good times, we will now look back and summarise some of these, at times, uncomfortable truths. They are our truths and may not be anyone else's. They may not be what those experiencing mental illness or their loved ones want to read, but if these truths are universal (and it's possible they may not be), it is helpful to know about them.

Depression can be random

Some people may experience mental ill-health because of what we might call external issues – issues with step-parents, bullying at school or on social media, childhood trauma such as the death of a parent or sibling, etc. Others, like Michael, suffer for no apparent reason. It happens. Life isn't fair. You just have to get on with it and make the best of what you've got.

It's not your fault

This needs to be stressed again and again and again. Someone with mental health is not to blame. Their loved ones – partner, parents, family – are not to blame either. There is often no rhyme or reason to any of it. You've just been dealt a bad hand of cards; you have to play it as best you can.

Depression changes people

Depression, anxiety and other issues often turn the sufferer into someone you don't recognise. You may not like them very much – and I think it's okay to acknowledge that. I do. For a long time, I thought Michael was not a nice person. If I'm really honest, there were moments when I thought he was ghastly. You may feel anger, despair, frustration, disappointment and all sorts of other 'how did we come to this?' emotions. I felt those and more. These are all natural feelings. It may help to have an image of that tentacled monster in your head – your loved one is still in there somewhere.

You're not a superhero

There's not a lot you, as a loved one, can do to turn what's happening around, so don't expect too much of yourself. When Michael came back, we were there for him, we talked, we bought a bicycle, a computer and art equipment and whatever he felt he needed, we went to the cinema a lot; we did everything we could to be there and to help and to encourage him. But I would not want anyone to think we were saints or heroes or that we saved Michael. We helped a bit, I'm sure, but this was Michael's journey, he pretty much travelled it on his own and he saved himself.

Resolution comes from within

Tackling mental ill-health has to come from deep down inside the sufferer. The old expression 'You can lead a horse to water, but you can't make it drink' is spot-on. Beg, threaten, plead, shout – it makes no difference (except to the relationship between you). I don't think anyone could have done more for Michael than Niamh, but she could not save him; eventually, she had to save herself and hope that the Maitland family could help Michael to reach an equilibrium.

Rock bottom comes first

I talk regularly to those with mental health issues and their loved ones, and I am sometimes asked not to say this. I believe the person has to reach rock bottom before they will decide that the only choice they have is to turn things around...or die. It's not a comfortable thought if you and yours are in the early stages of the journey. I believe it to be true; at least, it was for Michael. I think you, as a loved one, need to be there when they hit the bottom.

There's no easy solution

There is no quick fix. With lower-level issues of depression and anxiety – still terrible for the sufferer – it is possible that these can be resolved with some sort of relatively quick fix. A course of medication, some rest and relaxation and exercise, a resolution of or coming to terms with the issue may be enough. Generally, though, it's a long haul – Michael's journey spans from 2007 onwards.

There's no universal cure

There are all sorts of treatments out there and different ways to get to them, but what works for one person may not work for another. It's a 'pick and mix' matter: trying alternatives to see what works best in the circumstances. You need to be open to what's on offer. Some ideas – breathing deeply, chanting mantras, lighting candles – may seem nonsensical to some people, especially to those who see themselves as rock-hard tough men, but these methods have helped others to get better. Please keep your mind open. They work for many – simple as that.

It's always there

You may have to live with mental ill-health for ever, at least to some degree. Again, this is not something that anyone wants to read – but we believe it is true. It is for our family anyway. Michael, as we came through 2016, still had ongoing issues, with anxiety mainly, not to the point where he would have to go back on medication or need to see a therapist, or become anorexic, or go into hospital or the Priory. However, he needed to manage these issues and, to be fair, he seemed to be doing so effectively.

July 2016
My five minutes of fame

My dad's book has just come out and we have been doing a lot of promotion work for it with the papers. I did an interview with *The Telegraph* at home last week. My dad did one with *The Sunday Times*. Today we have been doing radio interviews in London to talk about the book. We've been on BBC Radio 5 Live and BBC Radio London. We also did a live interview down the line to BBC Radio Hereford and Worcester. My dad says that's another one off his bucket list.

We talk about the book but it's mainly about my past and what has happened to me. It's always really difficult and pretty draining for me to talk about that, but I hope it helps the book do well. We have also been asked to do *The One Show* on the BBC, which is both exciting and terrifying. I don't like doing this kind of thing very much but do it for my dad. I didn't talk to anyone in years and rarely left my house, so to be in the public eye, even for five minutes of 'fame', is daunting.

* * *

We have also been approached by a charity called stem4 and one or two companies who want us to give talks in different places – workplaces in London mainly. stem4 is a teen mental health charity and they are all about supporting teenagers with mental health issues like depression and anxiety. I think they want me and my dad to be ambassadors for them and go and give talks. My dad says it is good to put something back, so we will do that.

The other work is where we have to give talks to office workers in London. I'd have to actually wear smart clothes, like a suit and tie. Maybe one day the way people look at tattoos will change. It has changed slowly over the years but it's still not there yet. Older people look at me sometimes and make me feel like I'm a horrible person. I'm not, I just have tattoos.

* * *

Me and my dad just did *The One Show*. They basically came to our house and did interviews with us separately and then together. They also had us walking along the beach with Bernard and then had us sitting on the rocks. I think they wanted to end it with my dad staring into my eyes, saying, 'I love you,' which is about as likely as a UFO landing on Felixstowe Pier. He has put his arms round my shoulders for photos and stuff and says, 'That's all they're getting.' The publicity blurb for the book says it's 'one long love letter to Michael', so hopefully people will realise what my dad's like underneath.

The One Show was really not my thing and I still think it's very hard to talk about my past on camera for everyone to see. Imagine all your personal issues being spoken about for everyone to hear. It's uncomfortable and always makes me feel a bit washed out, but hopefully it will help the book. I want to move on at times, but I know that doing these sorts of things helps raise awareness and helps promote the work we do. I just have to do as much as I can without it impacting me.

* * *

The funniest thing about *The One Show* was that Niamh texted me the day before to ask if she could pick up some papers I had filled out for our divorce and I had to say sorry but we're filming for BBC's *The One Show* tomorrow. Surreal!

She wanted me to leave some papers out under the doormat so she could get them, but I didn't really feel comfortable with her doing that. I don't like the idea of her here at my home. So I will post them to her.

Most of the time I don't think about Niamh, but stuff pops up now and then and I realise it's still a bit painful. I try not to think about her and just get on with things. My dad has always said stuff about time healing and I thought that was a bit stupid, but it's true in a way. You sort of come to terms with things.

* * *

We've just seen *The One Show* interview on TV. We all sat round and watched it, but I don't really like watching, I find it awkward seeing myself on TV. I think it's also that I know people I know will see it. I hid myself for years and now people can see it all. I've had people come up to me and ask me about it since we've been doing publicity. One old lady came up to me in a shop and said I was so brave and hugged me. I kind of stood there awkwardly. My dad says people come up to him at really awkward moments like when he's having a shower after his morning swim (at the leisure centre).

HOPES AND FEARS FOR MICHAEL

So, as we moved through the second half of 2016 – a full nine years on from when it all began and four from when he went into the Priory and some 18 months after he had come back home to us – Michael appeared to be shaping up at long last. He was doing a little work. He talked to students, parents, employees and employers about mental health, and was getting out and about with friends. There were signs of hope. But I had some fears for him too. This was a timely moment, with 2017 looming, to think over my hopes and fears for his future.

I hope Michael can find someone to be happy with. Brought up in a white, lower-middle-class family in south London in the 1960s, my definition of happiness would have been marriage, two children, a three-bed semi, a nine-to-five job and fried eggs and chips on the table for tea at six o'clock. I know better than that now, but I do hope Michael can find someone to spend his life with and they can love each other. I think Michael deserves that more than anything.

I fear that Michael still has mental health issues. He has lots of tattoos – arms, legs, back, chest – and they make me feel ill at ease. I am an old white man – most likely hopelessly out of touch with the modern world – but I cannot help but think that the extent of the tattooing has more to do with issues of body image and self-loathing than fashion. Many (older) people find tattoos – to that degree, anyway – repugnant, and I can't help but think that this is the effect Michael strives for.

He is incredibly, spectacularly indecisive. If you suggest doing something in so many weeks' time, he does not know if he can do it (even though he is clearly free). If I ask him if he can do a talk, he cannot reach a decision. He ums, he ahs, it's possible, maybe, have to see, not sure what's happening, have to check. It may be that he simply does not want to say no to me, but I believe it has more to do with Michael's long-term issue of not being able to make choices. It drives me mad at times.

If we go out to give a talk to, say, students about mental health matters, it's often a three-hour journey from Suffolk to London, two or three hours there, two or three hours back again. Michael will not eat anything and that worries me. He says he does not have an eating issue any more and that he simply does not want to eat in front of people (other than family and friends) who know he has had a problem and who will watch him whilst he eats. I can see the logic in that.

My bottom-line hope for Michael is that he is happy. That, when all is said and done, is all that really matters. The fact that Michael still has some issues – it would be surprising if he didn't – does not matter all that much. These can be managed. There are worse issues to have than being tattooed, not being able to make your mind up and not wanting to eat in front of strangers who know you've been anorexic. I imagine he will always drive me mad at times, but I can live with that.

December 2016
Looking to the future

I've slowly started to realise these past few months how much better I've been feeling in myself. I first noticed it when I stopped wanting to kill myself, although that feeling seemed to just pass without me realising it straight away. I then seemed to stop having panic attacks and feeling so bad about myself. The depression and anxiety are still there, but I am managing them better now. Depression comes and goes but it's far less severe than in the past. I know how to make myself feel better - stay busy, see friends.

I still find I can get anxious from time to time - I don't like eating around people I know are watching me because they know about my past. I'm comfortable around friends and family, though. When I feel anxious at other times, I try to draw as this feels relaxing and mind-clearing in a way. It's hard to describe, but when I'm being creative, my mind is purely focused on that and there's no other thought in my head. Sometimes, I literally just close my eyes and put on music. I think music is very important; it is to me anyway. I listen to music every night when I go to sleep.

I also have all of the experience from my past now and I know nothing is ever as bad as you think it's going to be. I have not seen Suzanne for a while and I have not been on medication for a long time. It's funny, I don't always feel that great at times, but if I compare how I am now most of the time and what I was like 12 to 18 months back, there is a huge difference really.

I wanted to end the year by writing down some of my thoughts for the year ahead. I hope I can get some sort of proper job and find someone to be with. It's been a long time now since I was with Niamh and I think I might be ready to see someone at last. I'd like to maybe meet a woman again at some point, one that I don't end up breaking up with. It's difficult, though, because I don't have much to offer, living in my parents' spare room and not having a job or much money. Hopefully, that will change this year. I'm going to write my side of the story with my dad next year and that book will come out in 2018 and I am looking forward to doing it. More TV and press and radio, but I think I am okay with that now.

I don't really have any major issues any more, not like I used to do. Going out was an ordeal at times, but now I talk in front of lots of people with my dad and I can manage that okay. One thing that plays on my mind a bit, though, is getting old. I'm 30 next year and I am still alone. I see people around me in relationships, with children and houses, and I sometimes feel I'm so far behind and it makes me feel left out sometimes. That does make me sad. But I also like being single and being able to do what I want when I want.

I try not to really think about depression or mental health and I now just focus on getting better. When people ask me what I want to do, I always just say 'Have a laugh'. I think it's important to have fun; what's the point if not? I've got people around me who know what I've been through and I think they are happy I'm still about and more fun again.

* * *

I think a lot of my issues have gone or at least they have been minimalised. I haven't felt really depressed in a while now, not since last year. I obviously have little blips here and there, as everyone does, but I know how to change the way I feel now.

What helps me to change the way I feel are things like doing some work that keeps me busy, gives me drive and makes me more passionate. Seeing friends is probably one of the most helpful and important things. My mate Adam has been there the whole time and seeing him always helps. I see him more often now and always have a laugh. Knowing family is there is important too. I know I have people around me who care. I also just try to make sure I look after myself – plan fun things, eat well, exercise and let go from time to time. I enjoy going to the gym every day. That's helped my mood a lot. I meet people there too.

I also now accept that I'm weird and a little different from other people and that it doesn't matter. I don't have to be like anyone else. I think everyone is weird in their own ways. I now just try to embrace it. There's nothing wrong with being different or a little strange as long as it's not hurting anyone else and you look after yourself and make sure you're happy. Being happy is my number-one goal in life. I always saw it as being selfish doing things that make me happy. It's not, it's what I deserve. Everyone deserves to be happy.

AN UPDATE FROM THE MAITLANDS

2016 was a transformative year for Michael – and for me too. Michael improved steadily to the point where he seemed to be as well as he had been for a long time. Off medication. Not seeing a therapist. Doing a little work. Having a routine. Getting some exercise. Going out with family. Seeing friends. All ticks off a good mental health checklist. If he could add a full-time job and a girlfriend, that checklist would be close to being ticked off in full for him.

I had seen my memoir, *Dear Michael, Love Dad*, published in the summer of 2016, with a paperback following in April 2017. I had also started writing a thriller, *Sweet William*, which was picked up by Saraband, the publishers of the Man Booker Prize shortlisted *Our Bloody Project* by Graeme Macrae Burnet, for publication in hardback in October 2017 and in paperback in 2018. I had also started work on a stage play and had more thrillers in the pipeline.

Together, Michael and I were working on a follow-up to *Dear Michael, Love Dad* – this book you're reading – and did talks and events for stem4, the teen mental health charity, and went into workplaces to share the story too. Other books, including a graphic novel called *Stick Boy*, were in the pipeline as well. Working together was good. Michael even illustrated *Sweet William* for me.

Sophie was now working as a primary school teacher and was saving up with Glyn to buy their own house which they hoped to do by the end of 2017. Adam was doing his A Levels, completing them in the summer of 2017 and hoping to go from there into the police via a BSc in Policing at a university in Essex. He was still with Normal Sophie and they planned to have their first holiday away together in 2017. Tracey was still working as a teaching assistant at the local primary school but was hoping to do something different soon.

Bernard the dog was due to have a routine teeth cleaning at the vets at the end of 2016 but a pre-anaesthetic blood test showed abnormal results and he was diagnosed as having a fast-moving malignant growth on his liver with the prognosis of up to two months to live. Bernard, now 12, coming up 13, had been with the Maitlands since 2008 when Michael and

Niamh went off to university. I emailed Niamh and kept her updated. She was as upset as the Maitlands and so the year ended on a sombre note.

BERNARD WAS GIVEN TWO MONTHS TO LIVE IN OCTOBER 2016.

January 2017
New year, new start

It's been a while since I've written anything, so the New Year is probably a good time to catch up on things. I've been doing some drawings and stuff to keep me busy. I do some work for my dad too. He's been writing a thriller, and once he's finished that, he wants us to do a graphic novel together. Five or six publishers want to take a look. I've sort of drifted away from keeping a diary. I think it was good when

I wasn't well as it helped me to rationalise things in a way. Now I feel better, I think it might make me introspective. I don't want to dwell on things too much any more. But I am going to keep notes for the next six months (for this book).

I've been going out a bit in the evenings at the weekend. I think it's good to get out and about again. I have been seeing Adam and Toby so much more and they have been very good to me. I owe them a lot. I have also started hanging out with old friends like Scott and Ryan from school. It's good to have friends; they make such a difference to me.

I have started talking to women as well, which I haven't done in ages, not since Niamh really. I have put that behind me mostly, but I still feel like I have a real issue with trust. I think I find it hard to trust anyone really. I think it's because I am scared of being hurt again. It's really tricky because I don't want to be on my own but I don't want to be hurt.

I have started talking to a woman called Amy, though. Amy is someone I have just been speaking to on Instagram as we know each other through friends. She has said do I want to meet for a drink tonight after work, so I said yes.

* * *

I just got back from meeting Amy. I think she's pretty awesome and I clicked with her straight away. I got back and went and spoke to my brother. I always tell my brother everything now. I'm excited to see Amy again. I think we might go for dinner on Saturday night.

* * *

Me and my dad did a talk about what happened to me at a really posh lawyers' office in central London. It was a full room and we stood at the front with a huge screen and what my dad calls a clickety-clacker to change the PowerPoint pages. He gets flustered by that and asks me to do it whilst he talks. He says he can't walk and talk and clickety-clack at the same time.

I always get nervous with talks. I'm not good around people at the best of times. Talking about how rubbish my life has been always takes it out of me. I get asked questions about Niamh, and once it's done, I always feel worn out.

It seemed to go well. My dad does most of the talking and they laughed quite a lot to start with as my dad does a few jokes. Then the story gets darker and I talk about that for a while and then we take questions.

Afterwards, a few people came up to talk and seemed quite troubled and emotional. I think what we do makes a difference but it is exhausting at times. My dad says if we can change just one person's life, it makes it worthwhile. My dad's a bit sentimental at times.

* * *

I just saw Amy again. Amy has a little girl but she has been staying with her dad. Amy has said I will get to meet her one day. She said she thinks I'm a good person and would like me to meet her. We went for dinner and then went back to hers to watch a DVD.

I feel a connection with Amy. Something more than I even did with Niamh when I first met her. I've started to open up a bit but still feel cautious. Amy now knows about my past because I gave her a copy of my dad's book to read and she seems to be cool about it. She thinks my dad is funny.

* * *

I have been hanging out with an old school friend I hadn't seen for ages called James who has also had a difficult past. I have been trying to help him. I try to talk to him and keep him company. He's a kind guy, but I know he struggles with depression. He has tattoos too and I think that people look down on him because of that.

If I've learned anything over the years, it's that people are very quick to judge. I always like to feel I give people a chance. People look at me, and I've even had people tut at me because of my tattoos, but it's wrong. I feel like the world is wrong sometimes. It makes me angry at times.

* * *

Life has been good lately but I really need to find a proper job. I'm asking around different places and have emailed a few different tattoo studios to see if I can get in somewhere.

February 2017
A time of turmoil

I have been seeing Amy a lot. We are not a couple but we are heading that way. I have met her little girl a number of times now and we have all been hanging out. We go out for dinner and sometimes I go over and we all play computer games.

I have met her mum and dad. They all seem lovely and things are going well. I know that Amy is cautious about commitment, though, so we have just been seeing what happens. Inside, I do want something more.

This weekend they are coming to Felixstowe to meet my parents. She has said she is nervous about that. She has also struggled with anxiety in the past.

* * *

James has been gone for a while now. I've been trying to contact him but have heard nothing back. He does this sometimes and it makes me very anxious. I want to help him but I don't know what to do.

* * *

Meet the parents! Amy has just gone home after a really nice weekend.

I stayed at hers on Saturday night and then on Sunday we went to the arcades at Felixstowe. I feel very happy at the moment. We then went to my parents' house and Amy got to meet them.

My dad was playing with her little girl and it all went really well. My dad then showed Amy a photo of him and Adam and Peter Capaldi (the twelfth Doctor Who) and then pointed out he (my dad) didn't have a proper neck; his head sort of went straight into his shoulders. He then also told Amy she has a nice neck, yup lol.

I dropped Amy back home in Ipswich and my dad texted me to say hold on to this one. I said I'll try not to mess it up.

* * *

Nightmare week. I don't even know where to start. I just got a text saying my friend James has moved away. I think he may have moved back home to Manchester to his parents. He was a nice guy but has spent so much of life in trouble one way or the other. All I wanted was to help him. I feel sad that he has gone. I'm gutted.

Workwise, I feel really low. I need to find something that makes me feel happy so I enjoy what I do. I'm feeling lost again. I feel the waves crashing in. I can't let it wash me out again.

I have been talking to Amy. She is worried that seeing me so much means that she is spending less time with her little girl. I spoke to her on the phone. She sounded angry. She wants nothing to do with me ever again. I don't even understand why. I'm angry and confused.

Everything has come crashing down. My world is starting to fall apart. I've dealt with loss before. I'm off to see my mate Adam. He's always there when he knows things are bad for me.

* * *

I just got back from seeing Adam. I find it hard to open up around friends, but we were in my car and I just cried. I haven't cried in a long time but I just lost it. I miss James, I don't have a job and I miss Amy and her little girl more than anything. Adam didn't know what to say and he said that to me. He said he's not surprised I'm crying. He said he would be. We just sat there for ages.

* * *

Amy knew all about my past because she read my dad's book. My past is something which always has to be raised at some point. Some people do stop talking to me when they know about it all. Some are really quick to judge and assume that, because I have had mental health issues, I must be nasty and dangerous, which is so stupid. I've never hurt anyone in my life, not intentionally anyway, and even when I've been churned up inside, I've tried hard not to let anyone see it. I'm okay with that, though, because it just filters out all the fake people and the real friends and people that care are still there.

It's times like this when I think I'm not meant to meet somebody. It has broken me a bit. After so long, I put my trust in someone again and I even told her this is difficult for me and she said she wouldn't hurt me. But she left in the most brutal way, just like Niamh. It makes me sad, but even more it makes me angry. From now on I'm going to be very different when I meet people. I think I'll hold back a lot more. I'm not sure if I will ever find anyone now.

A WORD ABOUT WEEBLES

When I was young, there was a range of toys called 'Weebles'. They were little roly-poly, egg-shaped toys that you could play with, flick and push about. The sales pitch was 'Weebles wobble, but they don't fall down'. No matter what you did, how hard you pushed them, they would wobble but come back up straight again. Michael reminded me of one of those little Weebles at this time.

February 2017 was terrible for Michael as Amy broke up with him. There were other issues all crowding in within the same few days – including a meeting with one of Niamh's old friends who told him Niamh was with someone else and starting a family – but the break-up with Amy was the thing that hit Michael really badly.

Although it was early days, they had talked of going on holiday that summer and of, maybe, sometime, opening a tattoo studio and café together. It looked, briefly, for one glorious moment, as if everything was coming together well for Michael – his 'happy ever after' ending. We met Amy and thought she was a really nice person who appeared well matched with Michael. We had high hopes. I remember texting Michael to tell him to hold on to her and yet, almost the next moment, she was gone.

He took it badly and, for one awful, heart-rending weekend, we all rallied round again as Michael was in agony, texting each of us, and Amy, over and again, sharing his thoughts and asking us what to do. There was not much to do, although Sophie and Adam in particular talked him through it. Amy had blocked him on social media and did not want to see or hear from him. It was over and he had to start again.

And he did, with some wonderful news coming just a few days later. For one dreadful weekend he wobbled spectacularly and we thought he might crash down, all his old mental problems resurfacing. We imagined that he might have to start seeing his therapist again, maybe a GP for medication, and that all of this might send him back to square one. But it didn't. Like a Weeble, he wobbled but he didn't fall down and he got straight back up again. It was that moment that convinced us, by and large, that Michael was going to be fine from now on.

On the way up

I've just heard back from a tattoo studio in Felixstowe from a guy I've heard about called AJ. He said come in and have a chat about being an apprentice there. I've always wanted to be a tattooist but didn't know where to start or how to go about getting into it. And here I am.

* * *

I just got back from seeing AJ. I also met Tom who works there. They are both covered in tattoos, so I felt at home immediately, lol. I showed AJ some of my work. I think he must have liked my stuff because he said to come in and start on Tuesday. He said if I do join, all he wants is for me to work hard on tattooing. He wants to see me succeed.

* * *

I've just had my first day at Inkspirations tattoo studio. I met Lou who also works there. She's nice and friendly and a bit...loud. My job is to do lots of drawing this week and see if I can get any mates in to have tattoos done. AJ said his aim is to have me tattooing every day, filling my diary and making a name for myself. He didn't have to take me on and I'm very grateful that he did.

* * *

I can already tell that I've found something good here. What I've learned from life – well, my life – is that bad things come in waves. Some big and some small. But if you can survive the waves, then usually something good is just behind them.

You just have to survive the waves and hold on for good things.

I could very easily have given up after I lost Amy, like I did with Niamh, but this time I picked myself up. I feel stronger. I'm now determined more than I ever have been to be successful and be happy.

AJ has asked me what my aim is. I said to have a laugh. He said that's the best answer he could have heard.

May 2017
Sharing my story

The guys at the studio don't know anything about my past, and my dad and I are doing a local TV interview tomorrow that will be shown on the BBC in the evening. We tend to be wheeled out for local TV and radio whenever there's a news story about male depression or anorexia and stuff like that. My dad likes doing it and I don't mind, and it might help someone who sees it. But I am kind of hoping no one at the studio does. It's been nice starting afresh and people not knowing about all the stuff I've been through.

* * *

I've been pretty busy. Even AJ's surprised at how many people I've brought in. I love it and feel like I've found something I love doing. AT LAST! It doesn't feel like a job to me. My dad's always been a writer and he's always said you have to find something you love doing; otherwise it's just work. When I was growing up, he said, 'Don't be a man in a suit working nine to five.' There's no chance of that.

I've also started hanging out with AJ, Tom and Lou. I go round theirs for dinner and Tom and I go for nights out pretty often. I feel like I've made some good friends here, friends that actually look out for me.

* * *

Today, my dad and I did the news interview and it's now the evening and I'm back at home. The interview has just aired and I've been keeping my fingers crossed no one I know saw it

* * *

A text came through from Tom: 'So I just saw you on the news?!'

* * *

I went into the studio as usual this morning and it turns out they all saw it – everyone seemed to have seen it. Even an elderly couple I walked past in the street! Ah well, at least they know now and I can give them copies of my dad's book. I would have told them at some point anyway.

A TEN-MINUTE RADIO INTERVIEW – THE AIM IS TO CHANGE THE LIFE OF SOMEONE WHO'S LISTENING.

June 2017
Life's good, really good

Tattooing is going really well. I'm meeting lots of people and AJ has said my work is improving every day. Both AJ and Tom help me on a daily basis and teach me new stuff.

All three of them (including Lou) have made me feel part of everything and have introduced me to their mates. I think it's helping me a lot. I think I'm gaining more confidence and being more like how I used to be years ago. We have even booked four or five conventions this year and I will be going to some of them.

* * *

I've realised how far I've come. I went to town (Ipswich) this morning and walked past Niamh. I've only ever seen her once before since we split, when we bumped into each other in town. When I saw her then, my gut instinct was to avoid her, but I couldn't because we both saw each other at the same time. I wanted to turn and walk the other way. She came up to me. She looked nervous. She saw my tattoos and touched my arm. I pulled away because I felt awkward about the situation. We only spoke briefly and I wish we hadn't.

This time I felt nothing. If anything, I felt a bit of anger, but I just kept walking. I know she saw me because she turned to her friend and I saw her mouth 'It's Michael.' I had my sunglasses on, my hood up and had my tattoos out. I just kept walking. I don't think I ever want to talk to her again.

Incredibly, I then saw Amy a bit further on down the same road. When I saw her, I didn't know what to think. I didn't want her to see me and she didn't. I also felt a bit of anger rise. I still have mixed feelings about Amy. It makes me sad but also a little angry. I now find it hard to trust women. I know they can't all be as brutal as Amy, but what happened with her has definitely changed the way I am.

* * *

We are going to Belgium for a tattoo convention this weekend. I'll be sharing a room with Tom, and AJ will be with Lou. They just got engaged and will be getting married next year in Greece. They have invited us to go.

I have been hanging out with them lots and we have been going out quite a bit. I feel like a lot of people are starting to know who I am through them and it's helping me build a name for myself – a good name for once. Not just being known for being the weird one.

Well. I'm still weird but I embrace it now. I think to tattoo you have to be a bit odd, and we are definitely a weird little group, but best mates as well. A guy called Brad has also joined us. He has been tattooing for years and is very talented at what he does. I'm sure he will teach me some tricks. That's the good thing about working here – we all push each other and want everyone to succeed.

* * *

I just got my fingers tattooed – ridiculously painful. It says family. Family is important whether it's your mum, dad, brother, sister or your close mates. I have both a good family at home and friends that I call family.

* * *

We have just got back from Belgium and I've had the best time. We drove and I went in Tom's car. We got there in the afternoon and set up our booth at the show before going out for drinks.

The show was amazing and the evenings were just as fun. It's nice getting to hang out with the guys outside of work. I can't wait to work the other shows later this year. I think the next one I will be at I might tattoo. I think I will try to find someone I can take to tattoo (not my dad).

* * *

If I stop and think about things, my life is pretty good now – well, amazing really – and it's because I didn't give up and had support from family and friends.

I'm so determined now to prove people wrong. I want people to see how far I can go. I also think I care a lot less what some people think of me – those who don't understand mental health or judge me for my tattoos.

I have a select group of people I trust and they want me to do well. I've also learned which people are really there for me. My family has always been there, my school friends Adam and Toby have seen me at my worst and getting better, and my work friends are there as well.

* * *

I'm now just working hard but also having a laugh. I try to make the most of everything and take every opportunity I can. I go out more, see people and try to laugh more.

I also compare my life when I would sit at home not talking to people for weeks on end with now being in a studio where I meet lots of people and talk to people all day long. It's an intimate job and very personal, so you have to be good with that side of things.

I still have personal issues I struggle with, but I'm trying to learn how to deal with them. I also find it hard to think about meeting another girl because I'm scared of being hurt again – but you never know. Maybe there's someone out there, somewhere who's as mad as me.

July 2017

A STEM4 STALL, MUSIC AND A BBQ

'Well, this is good,' said Tracey, sipping her ice-cold lemonade.

'Mine too,' I replied. 'Burgers are great as well.'

Michael added, 'I think that smell is from my shoes.'

Tracey, Michael and I were running a stall in a hall at a music and barbecue evening at Farlingaye High School in Woodbridge, near us in Suffolk. The event had been organised by students and teachers and featured a hall full of stands from mental health charities such as stem4.

Our job that evening was to hand out stem4 leaflets about the charity and some information about its Calm Harm app, and sell a few pens and stress balls and bookmarks to raise funds.

We all looked down at Michael's shoes – black and tatty trainers really, the same ones he'd worn day in and day out for as long as we could remember. They were literally falling apart.

'You'd better get a new pair tomorrow,' said Tracey.

'Go mad. Get two,' I added, 'Then you can alternate them. They'll last twice as long.'

We both laughed.

The evening was a sad one in many ways – poignant anyway. It had been set up after one of the students had taken their own life in the spring. Various students and teachers came up to us, shook our hands and thanked us for being there. It's nice when people are open and receptive to mental health matters.

There was a real sense of community in the air that night, certainly plenty of warmth, maybe some love. Students – boys on their own singing solo with just a guitar, girls singing harmonies, a rough-and-ready group singing the Oasis hit 'Don't Look Back in Anger' – all took to the stage in turns to sing their songs. Some of the students and parents clapped along. A few danced. The BBQ queue snaked its way around them.

It all felt normal and fun.

We'd not had a lot of normal in recent years.

And very little fun.

'Sophie not coming?' asked Michael.

'No,' I answered. 'She and Glyn were going to help but the school had Ofsted in on Tuesday and she had inspectors in her class all day long and that's exhausted her. Probably for the best really.' (I pulled a face.) 'And I forgot to mention it to Adam until last night and he's over at his Sophie's house.'

A little girl of about four or five came up and I handed her a colourful bookmark. Tracey offered her a toffee, so big it could hardly fit in her mouth. The little girl took one, smiling delightedly as she tried to move it around without letting it fall out of her mouth.

'How's the tattooing going?' Tracey asked.

'Yes, good,' said Michael, 'My diary's starting to fill up a couple of months ahead and we're doing some tattoo conventions later in the year. Wrexham's one in November. Is that in Wales?'

'Duh. Norfolk.'

'Is it?'

Tracey laughed. 'No, Dad's joking, it's in Wales.'

A young boy strutted up, jeans, T-shirt, sunglasses. Lively. Outgoing. Invincible. I wondered if he had issues; such a bold front is often a disguise that fools many. Loved ones need to look beyond that.

'Great job, guys,' he said.

'Thank you. Take a leaflet? Calm Halm – it's a downloadable app for anyone who has issues and might self-harm.'

I could see him thinking, 'No, not me mate, no chance,' but he took one anyway and swaggered off, full of youthful charm.

'You staying to the end?' I asked Michael.

'I'll go at 8.15. I want to get something to eat from the Co-op before it closes. Then I'm going to have a drink with AJ and Tom and Nate.'

'Sounds delightful.'

'Why?'

I shook my head. 'We'll leave the front door unlocked. Will you need a bucket?'

Tracey laughed.

A woman and a daughter came up, both reaching out to touch the stress balls that were in the middle of the table.

'I'll get one of these for your dad,' said the mother to the daughter, as she handed over the change for it.

Tracey handed her a leaflet too. Perhaps if the throwaway comment was a sign of something more serious, he'd make a call, send an anonymous email, talk to someone. At least the family was aware of it.

'It's going to be a funny old summer this year,' I said, 'Adam's off to Amsterdam with his Sophie at the end of July. Then Sophie and Glyn are having a weekend in Paris at the start of August and a week or ten days in Tenerife or Lanzarote, I can't remember which. Me and Mum are going to Naples in late August.'

'I'm off to Blackpool in August for a tattoo convention too,' replied Michael. 'I'm not sure when.'

'We'll have to check dates, make sure someone's here to look after Bernard.'

'How he is now? How long's the vet giving him?'

'He's had the monthly check up and they're saying it's definitely benign and slow-growing. It'll do for him at some point as it will press on his stomach and he'll not want to eat any more. But she's saying six months to a year from now. Pretty good really.'

Michael nodded. 'Yes, that's good.'

The head of the sixth form came up to us to check we were well, had enough food and drink, and to thank us for being there. It's good to see more and more schools and colleges being switched on to mental health and introducing it into school and college life.

'Great evening,' I said. 'You've had a lot to organise. Do you need these? We've two left now.' I pointed to the two remaining stress balls.

She laughed, said she was okay. We made some more small talk and then she went off to talk to the people running the other stands.

Michael got up to leave, 15 minutes to go, everyone ready to start packing up.

He asked for directions. I pointed him in the opposite direction to where he needed to go.

'Are you sure?' he said. 'Wasn't it that way?'

'No,' I answered. 'Well, that way's quicker.'

He looked unconvinced but went the way I pointed.

'He's all right, isn't he?' I asked, turning to Tracey.

'Yes,' she replied. 'He's Michael again.'

I nodded, trying to think of something funny to say, but failing. An emotional moment.

Then Michael came wandering back from where I'd sent him. 'By the way,' he said, as he passed by, 'I've had a text from Amy. She wants to meet for a drink, have a chat.'

'Oh, please. Don't tell me she's five months pregnant!' I shouted instinctively after him.

Tracey added, 'Are you going to? Are you going to see her again?'

Michael turned towards us, smiled and laughed, and then moved off in the right direction.

At last.

Further Reading

As our book is part memoir, part how-to, we wanted, rather than have a long list of detailed self-help guides and academic text books, to include similar-ish books to ours that we have read and feel are of benefit to readers…

We Need to Talk: A Straight-Talking Guide to Raising Resilient Teens by Ian Williamson (Vermilion, 2017)

If you've got teens in the house, you need to talk to them regularly (and then some). This book takes you through the conversations you should have with them (and I should have had with Michael before it all went horribly wrong).

Depressive Illness: The Curse of the Strong (3rd Edition): Volume 3 (Overcoming Common Problems) by Dr Tim Cantopher (Sheldon Press, 2012)

This is a useful starter book – sufferers and parents will benefit from it – as it gives you a really good overview of depression and what it's all about. 'No one's to blame' is the right place to begin.

The Recovery Letters **edited by James Withey and Olivia Sagan (Jessica Kingsley Publishers, 2017)**

Letters written by those who have experienced depression (and come out the other side) to those who are currently suffering. Powerful and moving but, best of all, full of advice and hope for the future. Inspirational at times.

Overcoming Depression: A Self-Help Guide Using Cognitive Behavioural Techniques **by Paul Gilbert (Robinson, 2009)**

Michael's a big fan of CBT and this book takes you through it step by step.

Shoot the Damn Dog: A Memoir of Depression **by Sally Brampton (Bloomsbury Publishing, 2009)**

Raw, honest, painful, hard to read at times – but you will come out the other side with a better understanding of depression and how to manage it.

Reasons to Stay Alive **by Matt Haig (Canongate Books, 2015)**

A well-deserved best-seller, and described as 'an instant classic' by *The Guardian*. Frank, funny – it ticks all the boxes. You must read this, whether you're experiencing depression or have a loved one who is.

Boys Don't Cry: Why I Hid My Depression and Why Men Need to Talk about Their Mental Health **by Tim Grayburn (Hodder & Stoughton, 2017)**

Depression, anxiety and men – not a great mix. Things are getting better in terms of mental health becoming more understood by the general public. In our experience, women and gay men and transgender folk are more tuned in than straight white men, especially older ones. This is a book that should be read by everyone, especially (white, straight, middle-aged) men.

Anxiety: Panicking about Panic: A Powerful, Self-Help Guide for Those Suffering from an Anxiety or Panic Disorder by Joshua Fletcher (CreateSpace Independent Publishing Platform, 2014)

Joshua lived with anxiety disorder for years – who better to tell you what it's all about and how to deal with it? Some very strong advice to follow.

We're All Mad Here: The No-Nonsense Guide to Living with Social Anxiety by Claire Eastham (Jessica Kingsley Publishers, 2016)

This is a brilliant book – Claire has long personal experience of social anxiety, what she calls 'a crafty shapeshifter' – and really nails the different ways of handling it. We love this book.

Beating Eating Disorders Step by Step: A Self-Help Guide for Recovery by Anna Paterson (Jessica Kingsley Publishers, 2008)

Another self-help guide written by someone with her own experience to draw on and who has mixed personal commentary with how-to guidance. Parents and loved ones will find it helpful too.

Mad Girl by Bryony Gordon (Headline, 2016)

Depression, OCD – we love the honesty and the writing, so funny at times. It's a book I keep coming back to reread favourite bits (even for those who don't suffer from OCD, it's a great read).

The Mind Workout: Twenty Steps to Improve Your Mental Health and Take Charge of Your Life **by Mark Freeman (Piatkus, 2017)**

This book mixes cognitive behavioural therapy (CBT) and other therapies to offer 20 ways to get your mind thinking positively. Practical, informative and funny in places as well.

Dear Michael, Love Dad **by Iain Maitland (Hodder, 2016)**

The book that started it all for us – Michael's story, from my viewpoint, from 2007 up to 2012 (and a little bit beyond). It would be impolite to praise this, so we'll leave it to others. 'Wonderful, moving, humorous…extremely poignant', Charlie Mortimer, *Dear Lupin*. 'This is a wonderfully entertaining and moving book, with lessons for every parent', *Daily Mail*.

Useful Contacts

The key word here is 'useful'. We do not want to provide a never-ending A-to-Z list of organisations here that, because of its length, becomes largely meaningless. We would rather offer a shorter list of organisations, grouped under key headings, that we have dealt with in some way and are therefore happy to introduce to readers.

GENERAL MENTAL HEALTH
MIND

0300 123 3393
SMS: 86463
info@mind.org.uk
www.mind.org.uk
Mind Infoline, Unit 9, Cefn Coed Parc,
Nantgarw, Cardiff CF15 7QQ

Mind offers advice on all types of mental health problems, where to get help, medication and alternative treatments, etc. It's a good place to go for any mental illness issues.

RETHINK MENTAL ILLNESS

0300 5000 927

advice@rethink.org

www.rethink.org

15th–17th Floor, 89 Albert Embankment,
Vauxhall, London SE1 7TP

For general help on living with mental illness,
medication, care and treatment.

SAMARITANS

116 123 – it's free

jo@samaritans.org

www.samaritans.org

Freepost RSRB-KKBY-CYJK, PO Box 9090, Stirling FK8 2SA

Many services operate on a limited-hours basis; not so
the Samaritans. They're there 24 hours a day, 365 days a
year. You don't have to be suicidal to make that call.

SANE

0300 304 7000

info@sane.org.uk

www.sane.org.uk

St Mark's Studios, 14 Chillingworth Road, London N7 8QJ

SANE is a leading UK mental health charity that works to
improve the quality of life for anyone affected by mental illness.

FOR YOUNG PEOPLE
CHILDLINE
0800 1111 – it's free

Email via the website

www.childline.org.uk

Childline is a service provided by NSPCC, Weston
House, 42 Curtain Road, London EC2A 3NH

Children can call free on 0800 1111 to speak in
confidence to a counsellor. You can also log in
online for a one-to-one counsellor chat.

STEM4
enquiries@stem4.org.uk

www.stem4.org.uk

Connect House, 133–137 Alexandra Road, London SW19 7JY

This teen mental health charity offers how-to material
on depression and anxiety, eating disorders, self-harm
and addiction. Their free, easy-to-download app Calm
Harm is hugely popular, providing tasks that help you
resist or manage the urge to self-harm. We are proud
to be ambassadors of this wonderful charity.

YOUNG MINDS
020 7089 5050

Email via the website

https://youngminds.org.uk

Baden Place, London SE1 1YW

A useful website full of information and where
to go for more advice. Note that Young Minds
has a Parents Helpline – call 0808 802 5544.

DEPRESSION AND ANXIETY
ANXIETY UK

08444 775 774

SMS: 07537 416905

support@anxietyuk.org.uk

www.anxietyuk.org.uk

Zion Community Centre, 339 Stretford
Road, Hulme, Manchester M15 4ZY

Anxiety UK can provide help and support for those
with an anxiety condition. They can also help you deal
with specific phobias such as fear of spiders, blushing,
vomiting, being alone, public speaking, heights – 'any
fear that's stopped you from getting on with your life'.

BIPOLAR UK

0333 323 3880

info@bipolaruk.org

www.bipolaruk.org

11 Belgrave Road, London SW1V 1RB

If you or a loved one suffer from bipolar disorder –
what used to be known as manic depression – you
can get help and support from Bipolar UK.

OTHER ISSUES
BEAT

0808 801 0677

0808 801 0711 – youth line

help@beateatingdisorders.org.uk

fyp@beateatingdisorders.org.uk – youth email

www.beateatingdisorders.org.uk

Unit 1 Chalk Hill House, 19 Rosary Road, Norwich NR1 1SZ

Beat offers help and information on eating disorders, including anorexia, bulimia, binge eating disorder and related eating disorders. There is also a network of local self-help groups.

MEN GET EATING DISORDERS TOO!

Phone and email – contact via the website
www.mengetedstoo.co.uk
Men Get Eating Disorders Too, c/o Community
Base, 113 Queens Road, Brighton BN1 3XG

Charity supporting men with eating disorders as carers and their families. Check this out.

NO PANIC

0844 967 4848
0330 606 1174 – youth helpline for 13- to 20-year-olds
admin@nopanic.org.uk
www.nopanic.org.uk
Jubilee House, 74 High Street, Madeley
Telford, Shropshire TF7 5AH

No Panic helps people suffering with panic attacks, phobias, obsessive compulsive disorder and other related anxiety disorders. It also provides support for the carers of people who suffer from anxiety disorders.

List of Exercises